D1231883

City, Class and Power

City, Class and Power

MANUEL CASTELLS

Translation supervised by Elizabeth Lebas

St. Martin's Press   New York

Library of Congress Cataloguing in Publication Data

Castells, Manuel.
   City, class and power.

   Essays which originally appeared in French journals.
   Includes bibliographical references and index.
   1. City planning—Addresses, essays, lectures. 2. Social classes—
Addresses, essays, lectures. 3. Power (Social sciences)—Addresses,
essays, lectures.
I. Title.
HT166.C33   309.2′62   78–2978
ISBN 0–312–13989–6

Contents

Editor's Preface

The eruption of conflicts in cities on both sides of the Atlantic during the 1960s has led to dissatisfaction with the urban paradigms of the 1920s and new scholarly attempts to explain the relationships between social and spatial structures. The series 'Sociology, Politics and Cities' is designed to provide a platform for these debates.

The series focuses on alternative theoretical formulations of the social and political factors forming and developing cities. Emphasis is laid not only on single-disciplinary approaches to such understanding but also on attempts to build transdisciplinary ways of theorising about urban settlements. These contain elements of history and economics as well as sociology and politics.

Two types of book are being published in the series: small works containing reviews of existing theoretical formulations or excursions into new ones; and substantial works usually based on original research and combining both theory and evidence in the analysis of various aspects of cities.

The small books contain work on various schools of urban sociology and politics ranging from those based on Weber to those based on Marx. The large books contain analyses of many aspects of cities ranging from slums to ecology and from power to policy.

In addition to the theoretical and empirical analysis of cities the series also focuses on the problems of and prospects for intervention in the development of settlements. In many cases this engages a concern for public policy although examples of such private initiatives as shanty towns are also examined. Policies such as the urban programme, housing, race relations and planning are included in this vein.

City, Class and Power is a collection of essays written during the 1970s and based on empirical studies conducted after French Marxist philosophy had been applied to cities. The book develops two main themes. First, there is the application of a Marxist analysis of social class and the notion of the reproduction of labour power via collective consumption. Second, the relative ability of different social classes to use power to achieve their ends in the context of specific social movements or pressure groups is analysed.

Manuel Castells identifies the lack of a coherent analysis of cities based on the themes of social class and power. In doing so, he notes the self-imposed limitations, stemming particularly from American political scientists and sociologists, on the potentially fruitful field of community power studies. With rare exceptions these have seldom been applied to a comprehensive analysis of how different social classes get what they want in terms of urban resources.

The book develops these themes by examining the growing role of the state in the provision of urban facilities. This, in turn, establishes the increasing relevance of politics and therefore power in the struggles for these scarce resources. Planning is presented as one example of increasing state intervention in urban development. The ecological movement is given as an instance of the growing relevance of power and politics in the determination of urban conditions. A final essay seeks to draw these threads together in order to show the critical relationships between social classes, power and urban systems.

Taken together, the essays place a number of critical issues in urban analysis in the arena of scholarly debate. They demonstrate some of the ways in which Manuel Castells seeks to analyse and synthesise them. His work shows clearly that any satisfactory analysis of the development and functioning of cities must comprehend and take a view of the relationships between social class, politics and power in urban settlements.

London 1977   JAMES SIMMIE

Acknowledgements

The texts collected here have been produced and sometimes published elsewhere. 'Collective Consumption and Urban Contradictions in Advanced Capitalism' (written in 1973) was prepared for the International Seminar of the Council for European Studies' held at Monterosso (Italy) in November 1973. 'Urban Crisis, State Policies and the Crisis of the State: the French Experience' (written in 1976) was a contribution to a collective work on the state edited by N. Poulantzas, *La crise de l'Etat* (Paris: P.U.F., 1976). 'The Social Function of Urban Planning: State Action in the Urban–Industrial Development of the French Northern Coastline' (written in 1974) was part of a larger research project carried out in 1971–3 on the intervention of the state in the industrial and urban planning of Dunkirk. It was published by *Recherches sociologiques*, Louvain, November 1975. 'Urban Renewal and Social Conflict' (written in 1971) was based on a study carried out in 1970 of Urban renewal in Paris, and was published by *Social Sciences Information*, 1972. 'The Social Prerequisites for the Upheaval of Urban Social Movements: an Explanatory Study of the Paris Metropolitan Area, 1968–73' (written in 1975) was based on collective research carried out in 1972–4 on urban social movements in the Paris region. It was published by the *International Journal of Urban and Regional Research* in 1977. 'Ideological Mystification and Social Issues: the Ecological Action Movement in the United States, (written in 1971) was a report for the International Symposium on the Environment, organised by the Museum of Modern Art of New York in January 1972. 'City, Class and Power' (written in 1976) is an essay synthesising the whole of our problematic, and was published by *Le Monde Diplomatique* in June 1976. We would like to give grateful thanks to those institutions and

journals who made possible the production of the articles collected
here.

The author and publishers are also particularly grateful to Elizabeth Lebas for her work in translating many parts of the book and for her discerning comments on previously translated parts.

Chapter 1

Urban Crisis, Political Process and Urban Theory

The urban question and the problematic of the environment are in several ways at the forefront of the social and political scene of advanced capitalist societies. In the first instance, political conflicts and, in particular, electoral politics, which are at the heart of the decision-making process of the liberal democratic state have been profoundly affected by these issues. Parties often confront each other with different policies on urban development and 'quality of life', to which the electorate and, in particular, the new middle classes are very sensitive; new political groups and coalitions which centre around these debates appear defined by these problems. Thus, for example, the Italian regional and municipal elections of June 1975 were largely centred around the problems of local-government management, and have represented an historical leap forward by the forces of the Left towards a strategy of historical compromise enabling the exploration of the democratic road to socialism. In Japan the Left is in control of the large cities, and by campaigning against pollution and for a new model of urban development it has won positions at the heart of particularly conservative institutions. In France, the March 1977 municipal elections, won by a large majority by the Left coalition, have been particularly significant for two reasons. First, the ability to impose a political change at the local level prior to obtaining national power can be seen as an essential stage in consolidating a relationship to the population in the long process of transformation of societal structures. In addition, an important reason for this success has been the vote of the ecological candidates, which in the first poll achieved about 10 per cent of the vote in the large cities, and subsequently allied themselves to the Left candidates. This not only enabled the establishment of conditions favourable to a change in urban policy, but also reminded the Left of its deficiencies in this domain. Moreover, it must be noted that the ecological candidates did not preach a 'return to nature'; on the contrary, they put forward proposals related to the quality of life, housing, urban transport, public facilities, community action, nuclear policy, open spaces, linking them to the conditions of management and decision and suggesting local self-management, neighbourhood radios, self-help networks and co-operative organisations. The same trend has been observed in the United States, where much of the protest movement of the 1960s is now expressed as an ecological and community movement, proposing alternatives to local-government and urban development, and being increasingly involved in municipal elections where progressive platforms are beginning to obtain significant successes (for instance, in Berkeley, Austin, Madison).

The importance of the urban problematic at the level of the social and political dynamic is certainly not limited to electoral processes and the control of state institutions. It is revealed by the quantitative and qualitative development of urban social movements, i.e. movements which around protest concerning the urban and ecology, organise and mobilise populations, transform relations of force between classes, innovate cultural models, and become one of the essential axes for social change. For example, in Italy movements centred around the self-reduction of public service charges in 1974–5, the squatting movements in London in 1975 and in Brussels in 1976, Spanish neighbourhood organisations whose struggles have been a decisive factor in the ending of the dictatorship of Franco (1975–6), community movements of struggle and participation, which in different ways are developing in the American cities – all these are witnesses to the appearance of new forms of popular protest and organisation arising from the contradictions of daily existence in capitalist cities.

The direct effects which these movements produce on urban structures are less important than their repercussions on public opinion and the elaboration of urban policy at a general level, for their social visibility and ideological legitimacy are growing from day to day – the mass media often appropriate them, popular sympathy is easily aroused, large sections of the population, belonging to different social classes, feel involved. It is that which in a certain way forces institutions to take them into account and to engage in debate and negotiation.

Moreover, the city and the environment are also at the heart of the politics and, especially, the ideology of most governments, on the one hand, because as we will see state intervention in this area plays an increasingly strategic role in the economy and politics, and on the other, because it is through these themes that most often is considered the relation of the political with the material conditions of the organisation of everyday life.

It is from this fact that we must begin: the urban question and the ecological question are becoming some of the fundamental axes of social organisation and social change in advanced capitalism.

To speak of the urban question and the ecological question supposes both a differentiation and an indissoluble articulation between them. We shall now attempt to define their respective meanings and to characterise their relationship.

Neither of these two themes can be defined in terms of a problem of spatial organisation, for, if they do have a spatial expression (as have in fact all social phenomena), it is not this dimension which characterises them. They should instead be situated inside the network of social relations, their significance attributed in relation to the dialectic of social classes which underlies the organisation of society. How, within this perspective, can the urban and ecology be seen within historically defined societies, i.e. within industrial capitalist societies?[1]

Fundamentally the urban question refers to the organisation of the means of collective consumption at the basis of the daily life of all social groups: housing, education health, culture, commerce, transport, etc. In advanced capitalism it expresses the fundamental contradiction between, on the one hand, the increasing socialisation of consumption (as a result of the concentration of capital and the means of production), and on the other hand, the capitalist logic of the production and distribution of its means of consumption, the outcome of which is a deepening crisis in this sector at the same time as popular protest demands an amelioration of the collective material conditions of daily existence. In an attempt to resolve these contradictions and their resulting conflicts, the state increasingly intervenes in the city; but, as an expression of a class society, the state in practice acts according to the relations of force between classes and social groups, generally in favour of the hegemonic fraction of the dominant classes. It is in this way that specified problems become globalised, the urban question increasingly relates the state to daily life, and provokes political crisis.

In a certain way the ecological question poses the relation between human kind and nature, which in a sociological problematic is translated as the historical form of the relations established between productive forces and social relations, or, in other words, and on the one hand, how and to what extent, a certain type of social relations provoke at a given moment a regression of the productive forces, a destruction of nature, the two understood as the appropriation by the species of natural means for the enlarged reproduction of the species and the means of production necessary to it – on the other hand, how and in what way the particular primacy of productive forces gives rise to regressive social relations which threaten social life. This is the double facet of the ecological question which makes it meaningful: the double limit of the relationships between nature and society, between social organisation and material production, a limit which is not natural but historical, i.e. which does not negate the relation to nature but which requires the production of new social relations which can account for the *ensemble* of the demands of the material base and of history.

The urban question and the ecological question appear to be closely linked, together outlining a new axis of social and political change in advanced capitalism. In fact, their articulation occurs on several levels.

First, they are related in practice, particularly in the actions of protest movements and alternatives to local management and urban policy. In fact, when the demands of the ecological movements, the electoral proposals of the ecological candidates, or government environmental policies are examined, one realises that most of the concrete problems concerned are precisely those of the collective means of consumption which underlie the organisation of daily life. When one is agitating for an improvement in the 'quality of life', one is in the first instance referring to housing, transport, public facilities and open spaces, as well as to the forms of organisation of all the means of, consumption and their relation to other activities (production, management, exchange), i.e. what is generally referred to as the 'urban structure'. This has necessarily an expression at the level of spatial forms.

Besides, the management of the means of consumption and their relation to life style affects the other aspect of the ecological issue; that is to say, references to cultural changes, the progressive replacement of exchange value by use value for an increasing proportion of the population, demands for self-government at the local level. But the articulation between the urban and the ecological is deeper. If these two questions are linked in practice, it is because they have structural relations at the level of the contradictions which define them. In fact, *the urban crisis is a particular form of the more general crisis linked to the contra-diction between productive forces and relations of production which are at the basis of the ecological stake.*

For example, if there is a crisis in housing, transport, etc., it is largely linked to the forms of an urbanisation process which is itself the consequence of a certain type of relation between the social organisa-tion of human activity and the material base of this activity. The economic, technical, social and spatial concentration of the means of production and consumption responds to the logic of the concentration of capital and political management, and not to an adequate relation between the level of technical division of labour and social relations susceptible to the development of creativity, productivity and the human appropriation of nature in terms of use value. The urban crisis is the reverse of the uneven development of activities and regions. Metropolitan areas are only explicable by the desert of the pillaged regions. Overcrowding, the lack of open spaces and the creation of artificial technical environments are not the inevitable results of technological progress but the expression of a certain relation to the social and spatial organisation of activities. This relation is governed by the maximisation of capital accumulation – whether this accumulation be public or private. Now, this primacy of accumulation over social relations is itself a social relation, a class relation crystallised in a cultural model. Whoever wants to attack the roots of the urban crisis must deal with the ecological crisis, for it is only from new models of economic growth, spatial and social organisation that the problems of large cities can be considered. Without a transformation of the structural sources of the process of urbanisation, urban contradictions can only be patched up, for they rest on foundations which are increasingly untenable.

This leads us to a double conclusion: on the one hand, the structural and historical link of the urban and ecological questions and their close relationship to the fundamental contradictions of the capitalist mode of production in its monopoly stage; on the other, the direct political implications of these contradictions, to the extent that they can question the class power underlying the dominant forms of social organisation.

Having said this, the transfer of the conflictual and political repercussions of urban and ecological problems to social practices of change have none the less been largely perverted through an ideological encapsulation of the problems by the cultural categories and models of the dominant classes. Urban and environmental ideologies have indeed expressed the new social contradictions of advanced capitalism with force, but they have done so within the ideological terms distorted by state technocracy. The mechanism we are referring to is as follows: the social problems appearing in advanced capitalism are supposed to be produced by the forms of organisation of space and nature, which are themselves determined by the necessary evolution of productive technologies – the proposed causal relationship is as follows:

technological progress $\rightarrow$ urban concentration $\rightarrow$ social disorganisation; and also technological progress $\rightarrow$ domination of the 'artificial milieu' over the 'natural milieu' $\rightarrow$ derangement of human nature.

The above can be summed up by the following proposition:

technology $\rightarrow$ space $\rightarrow$ society.

The practical effects of these ideologies are very clear:
(i) Social contradictions are encapsulated. Problems and conflicts are due not to a form of social organisation but to a technological and natural process.
(ii) These problems become socially undifferentiated. Classes (as human persons) are considered only to the extent that the key question is that of the relationship to nature. In this way urban and environmental ideologies play down class contradictions and mystify the historical structural roots of the problems they pose.
(iii) The consequence of this way of approaching the question is that the solution to the conflicts and contradictions implied becomes technical, not political. Planning (rational, neutral and scientific) should replace social and political debate about the decisions which are at the basis of the concrete manifestation of these problems.

In reality this approach has corresponded throughout history to the ideological practice of the dominant classes. The capital–labour contradiction had already been recognised in the nineteenth century as a 'social question' by the reformist bourgeoisie who were more aware of the tendencies of historical development. But posing these questions, even in an indirect way, is a recognition of the new sources of contradictions, drawing attention to them and establishing the possibilities of political intervention, to the extent that they become recognised as legitimate sources of anxiety for most citizens. Then, despite the traps set by the dominant ideology in the formulation of an urban problematic, technocratic elites have at times nevertheless displayed more sensitivity to new historical tendencies than the dogmatic orientations of Marxism which have been locked into the sterile effort of reducing the social dynamic to that of the direct contradiction between labour and capital.

Thus the urban and ecological problematic arising out of the structural contradictions of advanced capitalism (even if in an indirect way), and diffused by the new ideologies of the dominant classes, is gradually becoming a central focus of the political problematic.

Now, this fundamental transformation of the historical parameters of the urban question has not been accompanied by an equivalent modification of the theoretical tools used in the analysis and treatment of these questions. In fact, the social sciences applied to urbanisation are still characterised by two complementary strands:[2]

(i) *functionalism* – expressed in particular by the great intellectual adventure of the Chicago School with its two theoretical orientations (Wirth and Hawley).

(ii) *demographic and geographical empiricism* – focused on the data collection of the spatial distribution of activities, using increasingly sophisticated statistical techniques but which are devoid of meaning in relation to theoretical categories and social issues.

Since the problematic of the city has been articulated to that of power, in accordance to the historical process outlined above, these two strands have been in a quandary.

The problem at the heart of sociological functionalism is that of social integration, and it corresponds to the need to integrate (and to class-discipline) the mass of uprooted immigrants into the productive machine of the capitalist city. The whole of the Chicago School, as all the founders of academic sociology, are governed by this theme. Now, the recognition of power as the fundamental axis of the city completely displaces the questions to be posed, and hence the tools necessary to answer them. The question is no longer to know how the social life of a neighbourhood is organised *vis-à-vis* the dominant culture, but how are to be determined the housing and infrastructural policies of the city from the relations of force between social groups structurally determined by their interests. New concepts and theories become necessary to consider problems of conflict and the decision-making processes which appear to determine the whole of urban organisation.

And we are here talking about new theories, for the forward flight of urban empiricism revealed itself to be even less fruitful than the intellectual constructions of functionalism. In effect, the social sciences have accumulated a fantastic mass of data and relations between data which have been unable to put forward any analysis which could go beyond a few *ad hoc* hypotheses or descriptions of particular situations which are always impossible to generalise from. True, these studies can be primary material for the reflection upon the real tendencies of urban development; but they often could have been more useful if their data collection had followed and not preceeded theoretical reflection on the given problem. The difficulty arises precisely because the theory is weak, and it becomes safer to gather a few bits of information, to use one's common sense, and to prove one's professional competence at the level of the methodological treatment of information. One could add that the replacement of statistical models by geographical and anthropological monographs only imbues empiricism with some human warmth: quantitative empiricism thus becomes poetical empiricism without, however, improving the possibility of a general theoretical interpretation.

There has only been one serious theoretical attempt to develop a new approach adapted to urban historical transformation: the liberal theory of pluralism arising out of American political science. This school does start out with the recognition that the processes of urban organisation are political processes arising from the interplay of power exercised by various actors. Both the data collected and the analyses arrived at are defined by the properly social and political character of the reality observed. In relation to the problematics of social integration and demographic empiricism, this was a great step. Having said this, the theoretical foundations of this perspective nevertheless invalidates the potential fecundity of the approach, for the pluralist conception of political theory only defines empirically actors in conflict, without situating them within the structural framework of the class interests which underlie them. The consequence is that either one stays with a description of conflicts in a given context, or that one implicitly refers to a liberal theory of social action whereby each actor, whoever he is (union, mayor, employer, charitable organisation or daily newspaper), attempts to maximise his advantages, these being understood as being either accession to the institutional system of power, or the appropriation of money.[3] One cannot derive any laws from these analyses, only formal mechanisms between actors; and these mechanisms are valid only as far as there is a common acceptance by the actors concerned of the political and ideological frame of reference to which social behaviour ajusts itself. As soon as alternatives are posed to social organisation, as soon as one is no longer interested in participation in the system, but instead in the contradictory expression of relations of power, liberal theory, centred around a subjective rather than a structural definition of actors, reveals itself to be incapable of accounting for the phenomena observed, that is to say, liberal analysis can only describe, not understand, the process of social change. Now, we have previously mentioned that what characterises the urban problematic in advanced capitalism is precisely its close relation to social change. How, then, can one use a theory which is incapable of explaining the social structural sources of innovatory behaviour? Beyond the world of strategic calculation (intellectually dependent upon the liberal economic theory of marginal utility), one would need a theory capable of explaining the production of new relations arising at one and the same time from the transformation of social structures and from the corresponding new historical practices.

In most advanced capitalist societies, the discrepancy between existing modes of thought in the urban social sciences and actual and increasingly political experiences has been realised. The first reaction was a refusal of all theoretisation, a political pragmatism, an affirmation that all knowledge could only come from practice; and this was the position of both the dominant technocracy and the political opposition linked to protest movements.

This political empiricism can be explained by the fact that a breath of fresh air was needed in the suffocating world of academic social science. But its limits were quickly revealed as soon as practice, in order not to be blind, had to interpret its experiences and to make new choices inside a cumulative approach of acquired knowledge.

Thus the pragmatic denial of urban pseudo-theories was succeeded by research into new theoretical tools, which *while founded on practice and experience* have the possibilities for a more general elaboration, allowing prediction, and as such the conscious orientation of action.

It is especially in France that this intellectual–political movement has grown in the 1970s, this for a number of reasons, all of which relate to the historical break of 1968. The large social movement of revolt during that period created conditions which were extremely favourable to the development of a new type of urban research:

(i) Except for the more entrenched posts of the Establishment, universities, and research in general, were largely won over by the movement of protest. Many intellectuals attempted to renew their work interests by analysing social change, particularly in its new dimensions (cultural revolts, the urban crisis, women's liberation, immigrant workers, etc.).

(ii) The general relation of forces in French society was upset by the social struggles and the political offensive of the Left which followed. This modification of class hegemony was expressed even in the state itself, in research and university teaching institutions. Large areas of freedom were won. Because of this, certain kinds of research which were unthinkable prior to 1968 were able to develop, financed by the state and carried out within public institutions, in part thanks to the progressive thinking of a number of civil servants.

(iii) The dominant classes, and especially the state technocracy, were surprised by the economic, social and political crisis which declared itself as far back as 1967. They immediately tried to understand it; and because urban ideology was one of its principal terms of reference, they translated the social crisis into an urban crisis, and attempted to develop research within this perspective with a freedom which was all the greater because they could not master the givens of the problem.

(iv) Last, unions, parties of the Left, the radical Left, realised, a little late, that there were new problems to deal with, new struggles to direct in the confused arena of urbanism and the environment. They then stimulated their adherents, intellectuals in particular, to interest themselves in it in order to construct a new problematic which could be an alternative to the urban ideology of the technocracy.

French researchers (of which there are a relatively important number) thus found themselves in a very dynamic social and political situation, with institutions responsive to a new definition of problems, and with fairly large research facilities in the area of urban politics. From this interaction between practice, theory and institutional research conditions there arose a strong strand of theoretical and empirical research which has within a few years transformed the mode of thinking on urban problems. There is certainly within this school a number of well-known names (Topalov, Préteceille, Magri,

Lojkine, Godard, Lefebvre, Querrien, Coing, Amiot, Cherki, Mehl, Mingasson, Kukawka, Ascher, Bleitrach, etc.), but it is as a whole, despite important theoretical differences, that a research milieu in constant interaction has created itself.[4] This milieu has a number of characteristics:

(i) While it begins from a strong theoretical base, it has developed through empirical research. Almost all the works written are concrete analyses of concrete situations which attempt to verify hypotheses linked to a more general theoretical framework.

(ii) It is generally related to the Marxist theoretical tradition, although the psycho-analytical and libertarian strand is becoming increasingly influential and in contradiction with the former.

(iii) It always begins from problems posed by political practice, as understood in the wider sense, by attempting to provide answers useful for action.

(iv) While being closely associated with Left movements and parties, the researchers have themselves insisted on maintaining their intellectual autonomy. Theoretical work has its own specificity in relation to political work.

This does not mean that French urban research does not have its own limitations: first, an *institutional* one, in that a counter-movement has arisen which has considerably curbed the resources allocated to this type of research; also, *political* and *social* ones, in the sense that urban social movements remain quite weak in France, thus inhibiting the possible revelation of problems arising through practice. In this respect this condition is gradually modifying itself as social and political struggles become important in this area.

Finally, and more importantly, there are theoretical limits, for Marxist theory, which is the major framework for this strand, has no tradition of the treatment of an urban problem. Because there was an immediate need for a theory, it was applied too mechanically, by adapting general Marxist concepts to the processes observed, without identifying those new aspects posed by the urban problems which necessitated new concepts and new interpretations according to the historical context. Generally researchers applied established theories without modifying them to the reality observed. In some cases it was Althusserian theory (Castells, Mingasson), in others, the state monopoly capitalism theory (Lojkine, Préteceille, Topalov), but the problem was the same: the theoretical coding has been too rapid, too formal, the reality analysed was more complex than the models used, which means that the researches carried out are far more important in themselves that the theoretical syntheses to which they gave rise.

Such mistakes were almost inevitable, but they can be corrected (always partially) because they have been made. What was involved was a redefinition of the urban question, empirical studies, a theoretical renewal and an invention of new methods – all at the same time. Perhaps the focus should have been the historical transformation of the urban, rather than the conceptual deployment of Marxist theory, i.e. Marxism should have been reconsidered through an analysis of history, rather than through the codification of recent history according to Marxist schemata.

However, the aim was to create an interaction between these two aspects, and on the whole it has been achieved. New research objectives can now be set, and new stages reached in the development of a sociological thought which is capable of understanding the role of urban contradictions in the process of the social change of our societies.

This information and these reflections may help to place this book in context. It includes a series of texts which are representative of what one might call the second generation of our work, i.e. studies where the recognition of a new historical perspective is more important than a formalist theoretical orientation. At a time when the initial works of the French School are becoming known in the Anglo-Saxon intellectual world, it is important to bring to the debate a few examples of theoretical and empirical studies, which while remaining within the general arena of the urban problematic propose theoretical interpretations of observed historical tendencies which do not always respect the hypothetical theoretical frameworks. This means that we are currently engaged in more lively studies which are more closely linked to the problematic and to a new type of Marxism, a Marxism rooted in the theory of class struggle rather than in the logic of capital, a Marxism which is more concerned with historical relevance than with formal coherence, a Marxism more open to its own transformation than to the doctrinal faithfulness to the 'sacred texts', a Marxism which must once again be a guide for action rather than a Talmudic repetition of ossified authors.

Chapter 2 attempts to outline the major structural transformations of capitalism which have led to the new role played by collective consumption and its relation to the urban problem. The aim is to establish a general framework for the analysis of the role of the urban problematic within the dynamic of the mode of production.

From there we focus on the relation between the city and power as an expression of the double dialectic of social classes, on the one hand by examining state intervention in urban contradictions, and on the other in reflecting upon the popular movements which have arisen from urban contradictions. In relation to the first part of our research, we first consider the general logic of the capitalist state in terms of the French experience between 1945 and 1975 (Chapter 3). Then two case studies on the intervention of the French state are presented: urban planning in the large industrial growth pole centred on Dunkirk (Chapter 4), and urban renewal in Paris (Chapter 5). In relation to the second theme, that of urban social movements, we examine the general conditions of their emergence beginning from the experience of the Paris region (Chapter 6), to then reflect upon the wider aspects of the ecological movement in the United States. Finally, Chapter 8 is a general synthesis of the themes considered, and outlines a general interpretation at the level of the current historical process in advanced capitalism. We will then conclude by a series of propositions aimed at developing urban research within the meaning implicit in the text presented.

The texts presented have indeed a strong internal coherence, but it is less important than the effects we wish to produce upon Anglo-Saxon research by communicating these works and the debate which should follow from them, for, if most of the experiences examined relate to France, the questions posed, and the way they are considered at the level of research, are similar to those we have encountered in the United Kingdom and the United States. If it is true that capitalist societies are progressively converging, it would also be advisable if the cultural and national barriers between researchers could also diminish – we must be able to help each other theoretically, for it is evident that the social sciences can confront the new urban crisis only if they accept the primacy of practice, the need for new theoretical avenues, and the overcoming of intellectual ethnocentrism.

This book, we hope, will be used as part of an open and urgent debate. The results are not indisputable, and, even less, demonstrations of a new and complete theory. They are research experiences carried out within a new theoretical perspective made necessary by present historical changes. Their limitations can only be overcome by a collective debate, which we are attempting to set up by presenting these essays.

Chapter 2

Collective Consumption and Urban Contradictions in Advanced Capitalism

Social inequality is the most obvious expression of any class society in so far as the place occupied in the system of production determines the distribution of the product among social groups, for, from the moment that we deny the inherent connection between the system of social stratification (related to the economic and symbolic distribution of the product) and the system of social classes (based on the system of production and, hence, on the power relationships between the classes), and make the former depend on the latter, it becomes necessary to spell out the specific form of this social inequality according to the phases of a mode of production and the historical formation of a social system. Thus the history of eternal disparity between the 'rich' and the 'poor', based on a fatalism with perfect results for the dominant classes, gives way to the precise analysis of the social production of differentiation at the level of consumption and to the study of the basic logic of a certain type of social relations which are experienced in the form of oppressive daily life.

From this point of view, in advanced capitalist societies one begins to perceive the importance of new forms of social differentiation and new contradictions upon which they are based, particularly at the economic level, in the still poorly defined domain of 'collective consumption', often expressed in terms of the 'urban problem'. Indeed, in so far as the indirect salary (i.e. the salary not coming directly from the employer but in the form of general social allowances) increases in importance, both relatively and absolutely, and at the same time as the conditions of life for the individual become objectively interdependent by socialisation and technological concentration (both economic and organisational) of production and consumption, it seems that the traditional inequality in terms of incomes, which is inherent in capitalism, is expressed in new social cleavages related to the accessibility

and use of certain collective services, from housing conditions to working hours, passing through the type and level of health, educational
and cultural facilities. This appears all the more paradoxical in that in
many countries collective services are reputed to be administered by
the state, with priority given to the social interest they represent
rather than their profitability from invested capital. But our hypothesis is precisely that, apart from the superiority granted by the highest levels of income (including housing and collective services), there
is a new source of inequality inherent in the very use of these collective
goods which have become a fundamental part of the daily consumption pattern.

These problems are treated as 'urban' problems to the extent that
residential agglomerations constitute the units of collective consumption and that their management is directly allied to the organisation
and management of the various collective holdings. Urban organisation is not, then, a simple arrangement of spatial forms, but rather
these forms are the expression of the process of collective treatment of
the daily consumption patterns of households.[1] This is why the 'crisis
of the cities' is profoundly felt, for rather than deterioration of the
'framework of life' the deterioration of the quality of life itself is
involved not so much of physical surroundings but of the way of living,
of the very meaning of life.[2]

This said, to go beyond a description of events and attempt to reach
the structural tendencies susceptible to more precise investigation, we
must take the questioning in reverse, not starting from expressions of
inequality but from the evolution of advanced capitalism and the new
position occupied by collective goods and services in this evolution.
It is only after this that we will be in a position to explain some of the
sources of structural disparity between the 'users' of such services.[3]

The Strategic Role of Collective Consumption in Neo-capitalist Economies

The transformation of consumption in advanced capitalism is directly
determined by the long-term structural tendencies upon which it is
based, i.e. the concentration and centralisation of capital and its constant battle against the tendency toward a lower rate of profit, the
socialisation of the productive forces, the development of the class

struggle, the growing power of the worker movement which extends its bargaining power to all areas of social life, and finally, and above all, to the massive and decisive intervention of the state into the totality of economic activity.[4]

Indeed, the search for new markets for capital is not achieved simply by the penetration of capital into countries under imperialist domination, but by its penetration in pre-capitalist or semi-capitalist sectors of the economy of 'metropolitan' countries, i.e. through dissolving the social and economic relationships which exist there. Such is the case particularly in the sector of the production of means of consumption for the popular classes, a sector until recently differing from country to country, and largely dominated by competitive capital.[5]

On the other hand, the class struggle and the growing bargaining power of the workers and popular movement imposes a certain level of consumption and changes the historical definition of 'need', both qualitatively and quantitatively,[6] so much the more so in that it is relatively easier for the dominant classes to cede to popular demands in the domain of consumption than it is at the level of production or in matters concerning political power.

Finally, technological progress produces several important effects in matters of consumption: it raises the capacity for response to the demands for consumption, thus permitting its expansion; at the same time, it necessitates, on the one hand, the convergence of this consumption with the reproduction of a labour power which has been rendered specific and non-interchangeable for specialised positions, and on the other hand for the large mass of the unskilled labour force, the socialisation and interdependence of production determined by technological progress requires the smooth functioning of the conditions of collective reproduction of the labour power (thus, for example, a specialised worker can be replaced easily, but it is important that transport assures manpower mobility so that several million workers can be simultaneously on time at their jobs). In fact, the more important constant capital becomes in its size and in relation to the labour power, the more essential its smooth functioning becomes in rendering cybernetic the most unpredictable element of the productive process, i.e. the workers.[7]

Thus we arrive at the phenomenon called *mass consumption*, i.e. the fundamental importance of household consumption, both for making use of accumulated capital and for the smooth functioning of the productive process, even when the production and distribution of these consumer goods is concentrated and achieved on a grand scale and when the whole sector is subject to the special interests of monopolistic capital. This latter aspect is the basis for the principal contradiction between the increasingly collective and interdependent character of the process of consumption and its domination by the interests of private capital.[8]

Such a contradiction not only conditions consumption, reinforcing the use of certain products (through advertising, styles, etc.) and determining the life styles of people as a function of the greatest profit from capital investment in such-and-such a type of product, but also, and above all, it provokes lacunae in vast areas of consumption which are essential to individuals and to economic activity. Such is the case, for example, in housing, socio-cultural facilities, public transport and so on, i.e. the whole sector which the economists call 'collective goods' and which are characterised (in terms of liberal economics) by the fact that they do not meet the price of the market, that they are not governed *directly* by supply and demand. Manifestly, this characteristic does not depend on the type of product (the production of housing is not more or less collective in itself than the production of automobiles) but on the type of capital invested, which is determined in the last instance by the relation between the rate of profit of the company and the average rate of profit in each branch. Thus we will see, for example, certain goods (housing itself) fluctuating from one category of consumption to another as a function of the capital cycle and the supply created by demand.[9]

It is at this point that the intervention of the state becomes necessary in order to take charge of the sectors and services which are less profitable (from the point of view of capital) but necessary for the functioning of economic activity and/or the appeasement of social conflicts.[10] Such is the history, repeated in all countries, of public housing,[11] but such is also the case for other types of consumption which are less explicitly public (for example, sports activities, 'art cinema', galleries, etc.)[12]

This intervention of the state is functional and necessary to the monopolies, even though it is often done in opposition to some capitalist interests. In effect, it assures the necessary reproduction of the labour power at a minimum level, it lessens the cost of direct salaries (for example, the effect of rent ceilings to combat high salaries), while at the same time easing demands. Besides, public investment, as we know, is an essential form of 'devaluation of social capital',[13] a major recourse for counteracting the tendency toward a lowering of the profit margin. By investing 'at a loss', *the general rate of profit of the private sector* holds steady or increases in spite of the lowering of profit relative to social capital as a whole. In this sense, 'social' expenditures of the state not only thus favour big capital, but they are also indispensable to the survival of the system.

This said, the intervention of the state in the production and administration of a collective goods is not permanent or 'normalised' in the functioning of the economy. It is always done in articulation with private capital, be it in making a sector profitable and in transferring it afterward to the private sector, or be it in assuring a continuous interlacing whereby the intervention of the state covers the functional or economic 'holes', thus making it possible for private capital to take over (thus the public highway infrastructure which makes use of the automobile possible, or urban-renewal operations which permit the actions of private promoters, etc.).

The massive intervention of the state in the organisation of collective consumption has specific and decisive effects on this, for if the state intervenes in the economy on the part of the interests of the monopolies, one cannot forget, on the one hand, that it acts in the interests of the whole of the capitalist system and not only as a servant for a given group, and on the other hand, that it has, *above all*, a *political* logic and that each intervention, even economic, will be marked by that.[14] This double relative autonomy of the state, at once in the interests represented and in the accomplished function, has two principal effects on the process of collective consumption and on the urban organisation which flows from it:

(i) It maximises the *regulation* function of the state, which will be expressed specifically through the process of *planning*, under the double aspect of a technical rationality and calculations in terms of social interests.

(ii) It *politicises* the urban question in that as the state is the principal responsible agent, which is to say, on the one hand, that collective consumption will be put directly into politico–ideological competition rather than treated in economic terms, and on the other hand, that the demands called 'urban' will be strongly articulated to the question of power.[15] Besides, the systematic intervention of the state in the domain of collective consumption takes on decisive importance in the current phase of capitalism characterised

by the *internationalisation of capital*[16] and, at the level of the daily functioning of the economy, by *structural inflation* which results from the
specific intervention of multinational firms. In fact, for floating capital
the taking in charge by the national state of the hidden expenses of
production becomes even more advantageous. Able to play on inter-
state competition, dependent on the goodwill of private investment,
multinational firms shift the responsibility for infrastructures on to
different local or national authorities. This mechanism is well known
when it concerns recourse to national credit, which has permitted
American enterprises to become implanted in Europe by borrowing
from private and *public* European banks. But although this aspect is
little studied, it functions still more clearly with collective goods, all
the more so since multinational firms (because 'apatriated') can be
less mindful of the social consequences of neglecting the needs of the
population.

Another phenomenon, namely, 'growth within inflation',[17] entails
still more important consequences for collective goods. Inflation, as
we know:

(i) hits the least-favoured categories of the population; and
(ii) encourages the purchase of goods already on the market.

In other words, therefore, inflation makes people more consumption-
orientated at the same time as it differentiates them according to their
capacity for consumption. In these conditions, two problems, *among
others*, must be resolved:[18]

(i) Important bottlenecks in the reproduction of the labour power
must be avoided, in particular for goods outside the market or those
for which the sale is founded on long-term credit and which are therefore made more valuable by monetary devaluation (housing among
others).

(ii) Guaranteed savings capacity in order to have available at the
proper moment new complementary resources must be preserved.
Thus it is necessary to assume differential costs of reimbursement of
immobilised capital.

In both cases public intervention in collective consumption is essential: it attenuates the effects of inflation for the economy as well as for
social relations while at the same time preserving the mechanism of

monopolistic accumulation, which is what inflation is. In fact, it is clear that the financing of this intervention is achieved by an increased burden of taxation which has a much greater relative effect on the work-force than on capital. Thus the gains in salary obtained by social struggles are not only obliterated by the rise in prices but counteracted by tax laws. Certainly buying power is increased by the combined effect of technical progress and economic growth, but the negative effects of consumption appear essentially at the level of collective goods which are necessary for private capital and which will be provided by the state and thus by the taxpayers. Then, one has only to blame problems on the negative aspects of urban growth, 'ineluctable gangrene of industrial civilisation', and the game is won. One can continue the epic of capitalist accumulation and develop individual buying power, all the while intensifying the contradiction between these grandiose perspectives and the historically dated reality of the *level* and *style* of life of people. To close the circle, necessarily individualised, personalised in daily life, in case of 'failure' there will always be a psychiatrist, or a policeman!

Let us, then, try to see the more concrete consequences of such an economic and social evolution of the relationship of social groups to collective consumption, limiting ourselves to a review of some examples, taken to be case studies of a general structural logic.

Class Structure, Urban Structure and Collective Consumption: the Social Determinants of the New Inequality

The processes of collective consumption simultaneously express the growing contradiction between their objective socialisation and their management as a function of the interests of capital, the contradictory exigencies of capital, the confrontation of the different factions of capital, and the confrontation between popular demands and the rationality of the dominant class to which the state necessarily subscribes.[19]

This group of contradictions forms the basis for new expressions of social inequality which derive from the importance of collective consumption in advanced capitalist societies.

(1) Thus in matters of *housing* the primary inequality concerns the income level which conditions access to the type of housing market, but it does not stop there. It is extended by economic and social considerations at each step in the access to a property, and this from the

point of view of housing as a product as much as of housing as a means
of social expression, or, if you will, as much from the 'quantitative' as
from the 'qualitative' point of view, aspects which are anyway closely
related.[20]

Thus the most common case in the United States, with a tendency
to be so in Western Europe, is for access to the bulk of the private
housing market to depend essentially on the capacity to have access to
credit. This itself is also a function of income level (excluding the highest strata), the *stability* and the *predictability* of income in the long term,
or in the last analysis on the possibility of a *career*, i.e. a predictable
succession of employment positions.[21] In effect, lifetime indebtedness
is the mechanism which permits the majority of American families
(but also Germans) to have access to ownership of their suburban
homes[22]. But the ability to predict employment is not only a function
of occupational qualifications; it also depends on the situation of the
business and the position occupied within the enterprise. Thus it is
that employment within large organisations and the functionality of
the position for the enterprise (and not for the productive process) establishes new cleavages. Still more, it is clear that this stability is a
direct function of politico–ideological integration in the productive
system and in the social hierarchy: one thus finds oneself before this
characteristic of the 'new society', and one is allocated a certain type
of housing according to the level of social integration.[23] If it is true that
there has always been repression against 'agitators', what is new is the
size of the phenomenon, made massive by the generalisation of
recourse to credit as well as the refining of the repressive procedure,
which takes place not only via the black list but also via the systematic
application of a banker's morality in the routes of access to housing.[24]

But the specificity of these new inequalities in housing is even more
clear in housing which is called 'social', i.e. public or semi-public
housing, and which arises theoretically from a logic of service and not
from criteria of profitability, for to consider the 'public' and the 'private' as two autonomous economic spheres is to forget the dominant
structural logic. In fact, the intervention of the state is accomplished
within the limits of the resources that can be mobilised, and, besides,
is distinguished by a subordination to the interests of the monopolies
in two ways: first, 'social' investments come only after direct aid to industrial enterprises has been effected; second, the constant tendency
is to make the sectors of public subsidisation profitable in order to
bring them into line with the criteria of private capital so as to be able

to transfer them gradually over to it.[25]

Thus access to public housing is limited by a whole series of criteria of selection (ability to pay rent regularly, aptitude for maintenance, size of family, etc.) which are also calculated on the private market even if they are put quantitatively at a lower level. The sources of inequality based on income, employment and education are thus reinforced once more in public housing.

But added to these economic cleavages are new criteria of selection dependent on the social and institutional organisation of access to public housing. Thus the insertion into the system of social security, though it seems consistent, leaves aside a whole series of situations (youth, the unregistered unemployed, the unrecognised sick and handicapped, etc.) which we lump together too quickly in a 'marginal' category, whereas they are in each case the result of a precise mechanism of social production.[26] Particularly revealing in this sense is the criterion of limiting the access of immigrant workers to public housing (in France they cannot have more than 6.75 per cent whereas they comprise 30 per cent of the construction workers); equality in housing is thus skewed and the allocation of public housing leads to new disparities.[27]

In the same way the ability to manoeuvre inside the bureaucratic network of public assistance in order to win one's case is a socially determined cultural acquisition and the ability to 'make it' is nothing other than the capacity for adaptation to a certain model of behaviour prescribed by dominant values.[28]

As a whole, these informal criteria for selection come from the very same model which governs competition for public housing; basically it consists of a concept of charity which could well be forgotten and which is addressed to 'little people'.[29] At the extreme of this logic one finds formulas such as those represented in France by the *cités de transit*, slums run by and, above all, controlled by the outcasts of the poorly housed, and where are collected all those who do not qualify under any criteria of selection (even if most of them are wage-earners) and who are left 'in transit' for several years, sometimes as many as ten or fifteen.[30]

Besides, in so far as housing is not simply a means to 'satisfy a need', but is a *social relationship*, public housing as a formula for privileged intervention by the state makes the style of life of these classes and income levels directly dependent in an area where they ought to have an escape from the economic and ideological direction of the dominant classes. Thus, for example, in France the delay incurred in the years after the war, the popular demands and the opportunity for a strong public voice instigated the policy of construction of large housing projects from 1954 on. As 'emergency' policy it was distinguished by the basic choice to construct the maximum amount of housing as quickly as possible at the lowest possible cost. At the urban level, this resulted in the building on cheap land, and therefore in the badly provided outer suburbs, of poor quality housing estates which were occupied even before basic household amenities were installed.[31] At the same time the image of collective public housing deteriorated because such undertakings were also generally associated with leftist municipalities. In 1973 the policy of making housing competitive, of extension of the market towards the middle class, as well as the renewed efforts toward social integration, through an urban organisation centred on the myth of the suburban petty bourgeoisie, led the government to forbid *by law* the big housing projects as 'negators of the individual'. Can one do today what was not possible in 1954? Let us say, rather, that the financial concentration of housing has become sufficiently consolidated to undertake the rationalisation and the extension of a new housing market over the long run.[32] Public housing is used in the same way in the United States, simultaneously as a response to urgent need and as a starting-gate to feed publicity for parcelling out suburban sub-divisions.[33]

Because of differential ability to gain access to the market, inequality in housing is thus reinforced by the inequality which results from the differential treatment of each class and social level by economic, institutional and cultural mechanisms of production and administration in public housing. Besides, each of these classes and levels is thus submitted to specific forms of manipulation which accord with the social interests of the dominant class.

(2) A similar analysis can be developed concerning the *system of communications* and the *organisation of transport* in large metropolitan areas. In fact, it is the division of labour which is at the basis of the complexity and importance of intra-urban transport systems, and from which one observes the spatial separation of workplace from residence, urban concentration, and the daily rhythms of the city. We know that such phenomena are directly produced by specific forms of social and technical division of work in a period of monopolistic capital. It is not a matter here of any sort of technological determinism, but a real expression of a social relationship. In fact,

technical progress is very often considered to be the basis of the metropolis. Despite all the arguments that we will bring to bear on this point, the role played by technology in the transformation of urban models is indisputable. Influence is exerted at the same time by the introduction of new activities of consumption and production, and by the near elimination of the obstacle of space, due to an enormous development in the means of communication. At the time of the second industrial revolution, the generation of electrical energy and the utilisation of the tramway permitted the increased concentration of manpower around more and more vast units of production. Collective transport assured the integration of different zones and activities of the metropolis, dividing the internal fluctuations according to a tolerable time/space relationship. The automobile has contributed to urban dispersion, with enormous zones of individual residences extended over the whole region, and connected by routes of rapid transit to various functional areas. The daily transport of products of current consumption benefit equally from such mobility; without the daily distribution by truck of agricultural products harvested or stored in the region, no large metropolis would be able to subsist. The concentration of business headquarters in certain regions, and the hierarchical decentralisation of centres of production and distribution are possible because of the transmission of information by telegraph, radio and telex. Finally, the development of air navigation has been fundamental in reinforcing the interdependence of the various metropolitan regions.

Thus technical progress permits, on the one hand, the evolution of urban configurations towards a regional system of interdependencies, due to intervening changes in the means of communication, and on the other hand it reinforces this evolution directly by the transformations created by fundamental social activities, particularly those concerning production. Industry is more and more liberated from factors of rigid spatial location, such as natural resources or specific markets, whereas it is, on the contrary, more and more dependent on qualified manpower and a technical and industrial milieu which stretches across the chains of functional relationships already established. Thus industry is looking above all for its insertion in the urban system, rather than for location in relation to the functional elements (primary materials, resources, outlets) which determined its placement in the first period.

At the same time the growing importance of administration and

information, and the liaison of these two activities in the urban
milieu, reverse the relations between industry and city, making the
former depend more and more on the complex of relationships
created by the latter. Thus technological evolution (in particular the
development of nuclear energy and the key role of electronics and
chemistry) favours the spatial regrouping of activities, reinforcing internal ties to the 'technical milieu' and diminishing dependence on
the physical environment. It follows that development starts from
extant urban–industrial cores and that activity becomes concentrated
in the network of interdependencies thus organised.

Finally, changes in the construction industry have also permitted
the concentration of functions, in particular functions of administration and exchange, in a reduced space which is accessible to all
parts of the metropolis, thanks to high-rise construction. The 'prefab'
has been the basis for the mass construction of individual houses and,
through that, for the phenomenon of residential diffusion.

Yet the metropolitan region is not a necessary result of simple technical progress. For 'technical know-how', far from constituting a
simple factor, is only one element in the *ensemble* of productive forces,
which themselves are primarily social relationships, and thus also
constitute a cultural mode of utilisation of work resources. This liaison between space and technology is thus the most immediate
material manifestation of a profound articulation between the *ensemble* of
a given social structure and the new urban configuration. Urban dispersion and the formation of metropolitan regions are closely allied to
the social model of advanced capitalism, designated ideologically by
the term 'mass society'.

In fact, the monopolistic concentration of capital and the technico-
social evolution towards organisation of very large units of production
are at the root of the spatial decentralisation of functionally related es-
tablishments. The existence of big commercial firms, with standardisation of products and prices, permits the diffusion of residences
around shopping centres, easily connected by a system of rapid communications.

On the other hand, the standardisation of a growing mass of the
population (salaried workers) as concerns their position in the production hierarchy is accompanied by a diversification of levels and by
hierarchisation *within* each category – which, in terms of space, gives
rise to a real segregation in terms of status by separating and 'labelling' the different residential sectors; hence they become a vast field of

symbolic display.

The ideological integration of the working class in the dominant ideology goes along with the separation of the activities of work, residence and leisure, a separation which is at the root of functional metropolitan zoning. The value put on the nuclear family, the importance of the mass media and the dominance of individualist ideology react in the direction of an atomisation of relationships and a segmenting of interests in terms of individual aspirations, which, in spatial terms, is translated into the dispersion of individual residences, be it in the isolation of the suburban home or the solitude of the big housing projects.

Finally, the growing concentration of political power, as well as the formation of a technocracy which assures that the long-run interests of the system gradually eliminate local characteristics, tends, through 'urban planning', to deal with the problems of the functioning of the *ensemble* by cutting them up into significant spacial units based on networks of interdependencies of the productive system. But this contributes to the regulation of the rhythm of the urban machine by the real functional unity, which is the metropolitan region.

The metropolitan region as a central form of organisation of the space of advanced capitalism diminishes the importance of physical environment in the determination of the system of functional and social relationships, annuls the distinction between 'rural' and 'urban', and places in the forefront the 'dynamic' society, the historic meeting-place of social relations which form its basis. We could address ourselves, eventually, to a major objection concerning this analysis of the production of the metropolitan region as a certain type of space derived from the logic of capitalism as a particular method of production and capitalism in a specific stage, i.e. monopolistic capitalism. Are there not socialist countries in which analagous urban forms develop? Then how can one deny that these are the product of a certain level of technological–economic development, independent of the principles of social organisation? Well, first of all, one must avoid approaching these problems from a capitalist/socialist dichotomy, which is not a theoretical category but a historic pseudo-globalisation which confuses and combines very diverse social processes. We do not use the term 'capitalism' to describe a historical reality which would be immutable and directly determined by profit in all social occurrences. We make reference rather to a particular social matrix, economic, political and ideological, which is determined *in the last analysis* by an organisation of social relationships founded on the separation of the worker from the means of production and on the appropriation of the surplus value by the only holders of the means of production. In posing this as a point of departure for the analysis of the determination of social organisation by capital, we have not said all there is to say on the subject; but we have said something essential because we can start from a specific hypothesis concerning the logic and the contradictions inherent in a certain type of urban organisation. It is this that we have outlined in our analysis of the metropolitan region, it is this which tends to prove the *ensemble* of urban research we have cited throughout the text. If in the 'non-capitalist' countries there are similar urban forms, that does not weaken the analyses we have made. Our analyses can only be discussed in relation to themselves, by referring to the methods which have been used to demonstrate that metropolitan configurations are derived from specific laws regarding the conversion of capitalist social relationships. In addition, such an observation allows us to pose a *problem* which could not be resolved except by means of specific research: the problem is that of knowing how there is reproduction of analagous social forms on the basis of different social relationships. The answer would require the following:

(i) determining if the content of these urban structures, their practice, and not only their spatial appearance, is effectively the same;

(ii) assuming that one does not confuse a mode of production with a political regime, seeing to what extent there is an articulation of different modes of production in each socialist society, especially at the level of the division of labour, and of course recognising the presence, in varying degrees, of the *capitalist* mode of production;

(iii) establishing the theoretical basis for analysis of a society in transition, for we do not yet have the equivalent of Marx's *Capital* for societies in transition;[34]

(iv) elaborating a theory of the determination of urban space by different types of articulation of the modes of production in a post-capitalist society in transition,[35] and being thus in a position to explain, for example, why there is strong urbanisation in the Soviet Union and disurbanisation in China, or, again, why the under-urbanisation in Hungary plays a very different role from that in Cuba.[36]

Thus we see that we are facing a very different problem that of opposing capitalism and socialism in general terms so as to unify them in the common semblance of some historically determined urban models. We proceed otherwise: we start from hypotheses concerning the structural arrangement of the laws of the capitalist mode of production in several phases and stages of development of this mode, and at several levels (economic, political, ideological), and in specific historical periods – which it is also necessary to take account of. Thus it is not a matter of finding a 'moral responsibility' for all social inequalities, but of studying the validity and the transformation of the social laws which have been established up to this point by research, by specifying them and modifying them if new observations require this. Thus, for example, the American model of the dominant class and middle class fleeing the city and leading to residential dispersion is in the process of being replaced in large European cities (but also in the United States) by a model of a quasi-village community reserved to the leading elite right in the heart of the big metropolis: living in new modern super-deluxe and self-sufficient buildings, built in the central city (very often in urban-renewal projects), working in the headquarters of established big businesses, and monopolising the leisure activities and cultural opportunities concentrated in the central city. Everything happens as if the delocalisation and internationalisation of capital is accompanied by a quasi-communitarian and strongly localised closing off of the executive milieu for whom spatial mobility then comes to mean, primarily, air travel.[37]

On the other hand, for the mass of wage-earners, the tendency is towards the growing spatial diffusion of activities, to the separation, more and more strongly evident, between residence, work, recreation, shopping, etc., and thus to an increased daily dependence on the means of transportation. Such a dependence sets up new cleavages and gives rise to new contradictions.[38]

The social predominance of the market, reinforced by the inevitable necessity for a collective response to the problem, is found in transportation even more clearly than in housing, in so far as this differentiation is expressed very precisely by the different means of transport: the individual, taken in charge by the market (even though only partially – automobiles need roads); and the collective taken on, in general, by the public sector.[39] But what is specific to this differential treatment of transport is the fact that for a large part of the population there is a combined use of the two types; this produces divergent effects, for on the one hand it generalises the problems flowing from the use of transport, and on the other hand it creates new cleavages according to the combination which can be made of the use of the two means by such-and-such a sector of the population.[40]

Each of these types of transport produces specific problems which come to bear on equally specific social categories.

Thus for *public transport* the main problem is its extreme dependence on the social function which has made it necessary, i.e. the daily travel from home to work at hours and locations which are extremely *concentrated* for the large mass of wage-earners who have no possibility of arranging their time or space. Consequently, in the same way as public housing develops at the minimum level which is historically, socially and economically possible, public transport operates at a minimum level, i.e. predominantly at the times we call 'rush hour'. Thus spatial mobility is worked out according to the time-tables of the big organisations, even when the urban structure of the large cities makes autonomy of activity in the crowded zones or districts almost impossible.[41]

This dependence on the time-table of collective transportation is reinforced by dependence stemming from the routes of the transportation network, itself also conceived according to the capacity to resolve certain problems of spatial distribution of place of work rather than the attempt to increase intra-urban mobility.[42]

One manifest example is the route of the new *Réseau Express Régional* (R.E.R.) in Paris, designed to connect the new business centre of La Défense (in the north-west periphery) to zones of heavy residential density of employees in the near south-east suburb, even when the growing difficulties of traffic in the suburbs require other priority measures (for example, the lengthening of various lines of the Paris metro towards the townships of the nearby suburbs).[43] The concrete result for the nearly ten million inhabitants of the Paris Region is to see the budget for public transport disappear in operations that increase mobility for only a special segment of the market of tertiary employment and only as concerns mobility for work.

Thus collective transport becomes a synonym for discomfort, for congestion, for oppression, for compulsory timing, if not, as in the New York subway, of personal insecurity. Then one thinks only of escaping it, of autonomy, of the capacity for individual unrestrained mobility; the 'need' is thus created and the market is there, all ready to satisfy the demand of the consumer – it is the reign of the 'car for individual freedom'. And once the cycle is begun, it is impossible to stop it. Cities explode under the weight of a traffic pattern individualised to the point of being absurd, congestion is a constant menace,[44] and becomes the principal cause of air pollution,[45] massive investments in road-building equipment grow continually without even catching up with the problems created, traffic accidents become accepted as a necessary massacre, resulting in a growing number of physically handicapped people. Technically, socially, the reign of the individual automobile as a privileged means of transport in the big metropolitan areas is one of the greatest 'absurdities' of our society. However, economically it is a necessity for the present structure of capitalism, ideologically an essential trump card for the development of the individualism and aggressiveness at the base of the dominant culture; here we have a concrete expression of what is called the contradiction between the forces of production and the relationships of production.

Nevertheless, the big car firms and the oil trusts have nothing to fear: the demand for cars, both in quantity and in quality, has continued to increase over the years, and despite the oil crisis does not seem to be seriously threatened in the long run. It seems clear that in the present state of urban organisation, in the situation predominating in public transport, in the framework of capitalist social relationships, it cannot be otherwise. The automobile, outstanding social absurdity, is at the same time one of the strongest social demands as a mythical means for individual autonomy.

This need for the automobile as a means for mobility, made necessary by urban organisation and by the way common transport is managed, is in turn a new source of inequality: on the one hand, because the level of income thus comes to order the capacity for mobility and individual security, depending on the quality of the vehicle used and the physical and psychological mastery of its operation (also socially conditioned); and on the other hand, because this extreme dependence on the automobile creates new sources of discrimination – all non-drivers are seen as virtually handicapped, even more impaired because intra-urban transportation is based on individual means. Such is the case for the aged, for adolescents, for housewives when the husband has gone to work in the car, for the sick, but also for the great segment of the population not equipped with a car: one forgets (bemused by the American image) that almost one French family in two does not possess an automobile – so many groups stuck in the underequipped residences, so many immobile people destined to consume little else but television, so many 'living dead', and so many future buyers (or thieves) of individual automobiles. Such are the everyday forms of oppression and social disparity in advanced capitalism.[46]

(3) *A new historical model of urbanisation.* Such analyses, even though rough and schematic, could be extended to other domains, for example that of educational facilities,[47] or 'socio-cultural' ones.[48] But even more significant is the generation of new social constraints by the very type of urban structure which unifies and organises the whole process of collective consumption.[49]

In fact, the big metropolitan areas characteristic of advanced capitalism represent a type of city qualitatively different from the city of capitalist industrialisation.

First, the different elements of the basic urban system are strictly connected and interdependent. Thus, for example, transportation and the localisation of its activities, equipment and housing, the centre and the symbolic signals, as well as each of the elements cited in relation to the others, form an indissoluble whole in constant interaction. It is not a matter of dealing with such-and-such an element of the collective-consumption process, but with the process as a whole; there is no longer the possibility of organising housing without intervening in transport or vice versa; there are no more 'urban problems' but crises and contradictions of the urban system.

Second, the structure and the processes of this urban system are directly governed by the logic of capital expressed in a specific way, i.e. according to the dominant function transmitted to each urban system by capital in the collective-consumption process (thus cities controlled by heavy industry or a centre of tourism will have their own forms of conformity to the logic of the capital which determines their existence). What is important is that monopolistic capital in the present phase is itself caught in a pattern of interdependencies, simultaneously by economic sector and at the world-wide level, and that it responds to a logic of long-term profit. This in turn implies the objective necessity for the smooth functioning of the various units of production and consumption according to a logic not accessible to these units but answerable only to the process as a whole.

Third, the intervention of the state in the domain of collective consumption, and the economic and political importance of the centralised regulation of these processes, determine the taking in charge of the units of collective consumption by the organisation. This is done by regulatory entreaties, more or less formalised, which correspond in general to the apparatus of urban planning. The cities of advanced capitalism are thus not only submitted to a rigid capitalist discipline but are orgainised according to the very requirements of the state intervening in this domain.

This is the completely new urban model that we propose to call *Monopolville* (Monopoly City).[50]

The consequences for the consuming agents across such collective units are numerous and complex, but they can be summarised in three points:

(i) Collective consumption and the routines of daily life which depend on it become extremely rigid, standardised and constrained. This is what we call the imposition of veritable rhythms in the area of consumption, similar to the cadences of assembly-line work in a factory. The personal sensation of tension and rush in life in the big cities is a concrete expression of this.

(ii) The *ensemble* of these problems appears as a coherent whole dominated by an implaccable logic. *Monopolville* is, in this sense, a completely totalitarian universe.

(iii) The supplier, the organiser, the interlocutor, the agent of central initiatives, appears to be the apparatus of the state. It *globalises* and *politicises* all the problems in making their collective treatment more necessary and visible, but at the same time makes their confrontation by the individual more difficult. The impression of powerlessness on the part of the isolated 'citizen' is thus increased. As a totalitarian universe, imposing the daily cadence, ruled by the centralised power of a far-away machine, *Monopolville* exacerbates its internal contradictions to the maximum, destroys all protective mechanisms and causes continuous strain in daily life to such a point that it becomes a fetish, a structure which oppresses by an ineluctable process. Such a process of alienation, in the classical sense of the term, reminds one of the making a fetish of money and the 'natural' predominance of capital in the relationship of men to the production process. Still, the contradictions and the inequalities created by this process are of another order and it is in these that the new sources of social inequality produce specific effects on the class structure of advanced capitalism.

Social Inequality and Class Power: New Contradictions and New Models of Change

We have traced the general lines of the structural evolution of advanced capitalism by showing the new strategic role which has developed from the process of collective consumption. We have shown, through several examples, the new contradictions which are born in the process and in the urban systems which constitute the real unit of operation. But where is the social inequality to which we made reference at the start of this chapter? How can we account for the class differences of the problems raised? The theme of inequality carries in fact an implicit reference to the relative positions of the agents. In this sense, have we really demonstrated that the 'workers', the 'employees' or the 'bourgeoisie' have their own relationship to collective consumption which is different from that of other classes or levels?

Such is the question we must pose in order to relate the analysis of the emergence of new social contradictions to the appearance of new forms of social inequality.

At the first level, the income, educational and occupational level dependent directly on the position occupied in the relationships of production, strongly prescribe the level and style of collective consumption and their relationship to the urban system. We have seen, in fact, that not only the capacity for access to this consumption by the market offered a greater autonomy, but also, and above all, that the internal cleavages of the 'public' sector were calculated on criteria of proximity to the market. From this point of view, one can say that collective consumption prolongs and specifies the social stratification determined by the class system.

But, aside from these effects of reinforcing the class structure, one finds new disparities, emerging from the historical mode of dealing with collective consumption, which do not correspond to the position occupied in class relationships but to the position in the consumption process itself, as well as in specific elements of this process and in the units of the urban system where it operates. Such is, for example, the case in the organisation of urban transport, discrimination against old people, or access to housing for immigrant workers (or for black Americans), or, again, the maladaptation of cultural facilities to the taste of young people following their differential insertion simultaneously into the schools system and the urban structure. Such 'inequalities' among social groups are not entirely autonomous of the class system since the logic of the latter determines the organisation of consumption, but the positions defined in the specific structure of inequality do not correspond in a one-to-one fashion to the structure of class relationships. It is in this sense that there is specific production of new effects of social inequality.

Furthermore, at a certain level it can be said that the *ensemble* of social groups are caught in the 'problems' (bottlenecks or contradictions) created by collective consumption and, in this light, if there is not equalisation in the result experienced, there is, in fact, a relationship which is not antagonistic between the agents but rather partakes (differentially, surely) of the same difficulties. Let us think, for example, of the problems of urban traffic: here it is a matter of questions which become obsessive for nearly the whole population. Also, if for housing the number of privileged people is larger, the crisis of housing largely transcends the frontiers of the popular classes – that is to say, in 'urban problems', social inequality articulates a question of more general scope: structural contradiction between the model of collective consumption and the model of relationships of production which is at the root of the class system, for the collective character, objectively socialised by this process of consumption, makes the crises and difficulties more solidified, less dissociable among the agents. Certainly one can escape from pollution and the noise of urban traffic if one is above a certain income level, but one is no less aware of the difficulties; that is, it is at the level of urban problems that one can see most easily how the logic of capital oppresses not only the working class but all the possibilities for human development.

This objective community of interests, this *partial* inter-class nature of the contradictions at the level of collective consumption, are the objective basis for the ideology of environmentalism, which tries to 'naturalise' the urban contradictions, welding the *ensemble* of classes and social agents into a single army of Boy Scouts unified by the high purpose of the preservation of the species. This also conduces to efforts toward social integration in the form of experiments in 'citizen participation' in the administration of daily affairs, thus reconfirming the old Anglo-Saxon tradition of the 'community' as an instrument of social cohesion which has stood the test of time in the service of the dominant structural logic.

But at the same time, the accentuation of contradictions, their globalisation, and their direct connection to political power, form the basis for a *practical* articulation of the more general demands for

transformation of the societal model. Thus it is that the growing
emergence of what are called *urban social movements* in advanced capitalist societies is a major element of the social dynamic in so far as they
permit the progressive formation of an anti-capitalist alliance upon a
much broader objective basis than that of the specific interests of the
proletariat or than the contingent political alliances.[51]

If the stated contradictions at the level of collective consumption do
not correspond exactly with those springing directly from the relationships of production, it is essential to understand the gestation of
these contradictions, beginning with the dominant logic of monopolistic capital. Analysis in terms of class is thus depersonalised and one
can speak of the domination of capital without referring necessarily to
the consuming habits of the bourgeoisie. It is at just that historical
moment that capital progressively loses any concrete incarnation,
that its logic becomes diffused on the world scale, that its power is
increasingly identified with that of world-wide political powers,
that the conditions are ripe for a collective realisation of the
obstacle represented by the social relationships structurally dominated by production for the qualitative transformation of the societal
model, but made necessary nevertheless by the transformation of productive forces and the forward leaps of political and ideological practice.

Some people will speak then of stopping growth and returning to
nature. Caught between their awareness of the crisis and their class
membership, they will choose the flight into utopia.

Others, by contrast, will find in the appearance of these new contradictions a field of choice in which to incorporate the great majority
of the people in the political battle against capitalism, the only real
historical practice leading to a qualitative transformation of social relationships of production which are the basis for the expressions, old
and new, of social inequality.

Chapter 3

Urban Crisis, State Policies and the Crisis of the State: the French Experience

Urban contradictions are increasingly becoming of central political importance in the majority of advanced capitalist societies; but this historical tendency has given rise to radically opposed theoretical interpretations which lead to very different political projects. For some, the problems of the 'quality of life' are substitutes for the contradiction between capital and labour as they become new causes of social antagonism.[1] For others, urban contradictions are only one expression among others of the class struggle between the bourgeoisie and the working class.[2] In reality, the research we have carried out[3] seems to show a series of new contradictions, linked to the present stage of capitalism, which play a new role in the political class struggle. In this sense they are marked and defined by the logic of capital – capital as a *social relationship* and not as an incarnation of the power of money. On the other hand, if urban problems are indeed the result of the development of contradictions structurally rooted in the economic and political interests of capital (and thus of the bourgeoisie), they do not rest on a direct contradiction between the bourgeoisie and the working class, but between the interests of the bourgeoisie and those of the popular classes, who both submit to the mode of organisation of daily life imposed by the logic of capital. It is precisely this multi-class character of urban contradictions which makes them strategically fundamental for a transformation of social relations, for they objectively generalise the sources of opposition to the dominant class for the great mass of the people.

This said, what does one precisely mean by 'urban contradictions'? And what are the processes of development of capitalism which have made them so acute and so politicised? On the first point, it is not necessary to re-open the debate on the critique of the ideological problem of the city,[4] but simply to recall that in most cases it refers to two series of problems: on the one hand those concerning the organisation of space, the social and technical division of territory; and on the other hand those which flow from the production, distribution and management of the collective means of consumption (such as, in general, housing, education, health, transportation and collective facilities). *Our first hypothesis is that the transformation of the social and political role of 'urban' problems expresses above all the deepening of the contradictions in the collective-consumption sector,* even if that has direct repercussions on the spatial organisation of the totality of activities which frequently leads to understanding these contradictions as spatial problems.

But we have also noted the fact that these problems are increasingly linked to political processes. The reason seems to be, and this is *our second hypothesis, that the production, distribution and management of these collective means of consumption increasingly depend upon direct or indirect state intervention.* From the point of view of the evolution of the state, this permits us to note that one of the fundamental roles of the monopoly-capitalist state is to assure the essential elements of the process of reproduction of the labour power, in particular in the domain of collective consumption.[5]

This chapter attempts to develop and clarify these two hypotheses and to investigate what theoretical and political consequences they may have for the dynamics of the state and class struggle. For that, we must reiterate briefly the connections between those processes which give rise to state intervention at the level of the urban. We can then propose an analytical scheme for understanding this intervention which will be illustrated with an analysis of the evolution of urban policies in France. Finally, we will attempt to expand the problem, taking into consideration the role of urban policies and struggles in the crisis of the state.

Capitalist Development and Collective Consumption

To understand the majority of problems which are called 'urban', it is necessary to begin with a study of the historical tendencies of the capitalist mode of production and their relation to the questions so raised. One can describe in a somewhat schematic fashion the development of urban contradictions by the articulation of several traits of economic and social evolution.

(1) *The concentration of capital* is expressed simultaneously by the

concentration and centralisation of the units of management and the means of production. Taking place in a process of uneven development, it has dissolved relatively backward productive forces and has concentrated the more advanced forms into complex units of production,[6] which, for the most part, have become preferential markets, and as a consequence, important exchange points.

Uneven development is translated into regional disequilibria, and the monopoly-capital accumulation processes in turn produce the concentration of production and circulation processes in large metropolitan regions. Thus follows the objective socialisation of the means of production, while remaining subordinate to the logic of the private profit.

The concentration of the means of production and the formation of complex units of production also involves the concentration of the labour power, and consequently the concentration of the means of reproduction of this labour power, i.e. the means of consumption. These means of consumption are in part for private use and in part for collective use. The collective use is determined both by the objective socialisation of the process of consumption and by the public management of these goods and services.[7] There is in fact a growing dependence of private consumption on collective consumption. Thus, for example, the use of cars as a means of transportation is determined by the layout of roads as well as by whether public transport is available as a viable alternative. Furthermore, cultural consumption practices are largely dependent on the previous access of separate social groups to various educational opportunities, as well as to the place they occupy in the segregated organisation of residential space and collective equipment. In brief, the concentration of capital results in that of the means of production and units of management, which determines the concentration of the labour power, and thus the objective socialisation of its reproduction process. Such are the structural bases both of the formation of the large cities and the necessary development of the collective means of consumption.

(2) But *the evolution of capitalism* at the monopoly stage does not only involve production; it also provokes a profound transformation in the process of realisation of profit. We know that one of the fundamental contradictions of capitalist growth is a tendency towards stagnation as a result of the shrinking of viable markets in relation to the growing mass of capital which must be put to productive use. Thus the stimulation of consumption plays a fundamental role in the total circulation

of capital in the monopoly stage. From this point of view also, besides advertising, easier credit facilities and a general increase in purchasing power, the organisation of the means of collective consumption becomes essential for the growth of individual commodity consumption. Thus, for example, we know the role of the American suburbs in the stimulation of consumption: each single family house becomes a self-sufficient universe folded in on itself and equipped with the whole gamut of appliances following practically unending progression. But the American single family residential model, itself the basis of a mode of living which is extremely favourable to the growth of market consumption, cannot exist without housing policies which facilitate home-ownership, and without expansion of the urban highway network, that is to say, by two elements made possible by state intervention in the sphere of collective consumption.

(3) *The evolution of productive forces*, structured by capitalist social relations, also determines the growing role of the reproduction of the labour force in the production process. This recurs in two ways: (i) for the very qualified labour power, to the extent that their productive capacities depend less on a particular action than on the mobilisation of the totality of their intellectual capacities, the life styles and general social factors must be considered as elements having a substantial influence on the process of production itself; (ii) for the unskilled labour force, it involves, above all, the contradiction between the objective socialisation of its process of reproduction and the individualisation of the decisions which concern its utilisation. For example, in a metropolis a large proportion of workers must start work each day at the same time because of the organisation of the production process. But the location of enterprises, or similarly the organisation of transportation, is not a function of this imperative, which creates bottlenecks in the system of exchange. The socialisation of the process of reproduction of the labour power at the level of agglomeration structurally requires a socialisation of the organisation and management of the means of this reproduction, contradictory with capitalist profit. Thus for the whole of the labour power, the evolution of the productive forces has had the following effects: on the one hand, the increase in the organic composition of capital and the interdependence of production processes (sometimes world-wide) has meant that the labour force has put to productive use an increasing proportion of capital to labour, while on the other hand, it has also become the least element in a production process which, because of the complexity of

its technical and economic interdependencies, must be in continuous operation to be profitable. Thus the evolution of the productive forces increases the role of the labour power in the process of producing value, and as a result renders the system more sensitive to the requirements of reproducing this labour power. This reinforces the strategic role in the collective means of reproducing this labour power.

(4) *The development of the class struggle*, and, in particular, the growth of the power of the workers' movement, has permitted an expansion of popular needs,[8] both in terms of the aspirations of the workers and the *demands* which result. The socialisation of consumption is thus accompanied by a growing organisation and mobilisation of the popular masses in relation to the collective means of consumption and the apparatuses charged with their management, particularly at a municipal level.[9] These demands are expressed on the one hand through the union movement organised at the place of production, and on the other hand by new means of mass organisation which have gradually constituted a complete network of movements in the sphere of collective consumption, from associations of tenants to committees of transport users. Thus the evolution of capital, the units of production, the process of circulation, the productive forces, the class struggle and popular demands have had major effects on the reproduction of the labour power, in the growing role of the indirect wage (price and quality of the collective means of consumption and social transfers) compared to the direct wage distributed by the employer.[10] Analysing the evolution by category of the annual consumption *per capita*, in France, between 1950 and 1970, one can observe a stronger increase than the mean in housing, in 'culture and recreation', 'transportation and telecommunication' and 'hygiene and health', the categories comprising the almost totality of what one would call the collective means of consumption.

This growth in the importance of the collective means of consumption in the family budget (and above all in the working-class family) is in contradiction with the capitalist character of the production and management of these means of consumption, for, in general, the profit rate for capital invested in their production is lower than the mean level, at least to the extent that massive public financial intervention has not created conditions of profitability. Such a characteristic is not inherent; it is a *historical fact* and, consequently, varies according to the country, the context, the type of goods. Thus, for example, one cannot include all housing under this rubric; it includes popular housing (and not only public housing) especially as the state has not succeeded in creating the conditions for a profitable mass housing market. But in a sense one can say that the largest part of socialised consumption requires intervention external to private capital, so that this partially transforms it into an object for marketable production.[11]

Thus one can note a fundamental contradiction in advanced capitalism between, on the one hand, the fact that the collective means of consumption (at the base of the organisation of the city) are required by capital for adequate reproduction of the labour power and are demanded by the popular masses, and on the other hand the fact that they are generally unprofitable in capitalist production.[12] The historical attempt to overcome this contradiction is the decisive intervention of the state in the production, distribution and management of the collective means of consumption, and consequently in the organisation and functioning of the urban unit which results in the articulation of the *ensemble* of these means (housing, schools, health, cultural facilities, transport, etc.) This intervention is marked by two social sources: by the technological and economic requirements of capital; and by the development of popular demands. This intervention is direct and indirect, i.e. through budgetary action and administrative measures on the one hand, and through economic and social mechanisms having a mediated effect on the reproduction of the labour force on the other. Taking a very approximate indicator of the evolution of state intervention, such as public expenditures by category, expressed as a percentage of national revenue, we see a clear reversal in the importance of traditional functions (political and military) compared to new functions (collective means of consumption and direct aide to enterprises). We reaggregate expenditure on administration and defence as traditional functions; and we class as 'collective means of consumption' expenditure on education and culture, social welfare, transport, housing and urbanisation and, finally, direct aid to enterprises composed of expenditure in agriculture, commerce and industry. Thus, between 1872 and 1971 state expenditure linked to traditional political functions grew from 5·0 per cent of the G.N.P. to 9·9 per cent; expenditure for aid to industry, from 0 per cent to 2·9 per cent; and expenditure regrouped under the rubric of 'collective means of consumption' from 1·0 per cent to 14·1 per cent.[13] Also, state intervention has considerably extended itself in the area of collective facilities and urban organisation.[14] This state intervention is not a mechanism for automatic regulation of contradictions, because, the action of the state is the result of political processes expressing class struggle.[15]

Consequently, it is not possible to interpret this evolution in a linear fashion. There are considerable historical inflections which are a function of the relation of power between classes, their orientations, conflicts and alliances. Thus, for example, Table 1 shows a clear deceleration in the 1956–71 period in state expenses for housing and urbanisation, while they grew enormously between 1947 and 1956. This is why an analysis of the social processes underlying state intervention which moves beyond an economistic vision of the almost 'natural' inevitability of the expansion of the state's economic functions in monopoly capitalism is required.

What is more important is that state intervention in collective consumption politicises the totality of urban contradictions, transforms the state into a manager of the equipment of daily life, and globalises and politicises the conflicts which emerge in this sphere.

Determined by the capitalist contradictions in the reproduction of the labour power and modulated by the political class struggle underlying national policies, state intervention at the urban level, which attempts to be a regulating element, becomes a new source of contradictions at the level of the popular strata. Thus it expresses, and at the same time accelerates, the crisis of the capitalist state.

Class, State and Urban Policies: France, 1947–75

Writing in 1976, one begins to understand the strategic role of state intervention in the process of reproducing labour power – which underlies the urban question.[16] But it is necessary now to specify the theoretical and practical questions that one poses in this context, to delimit clearly the analytic perspective that one adopts. In the study of urban politics the risk exists in moving from a reification of space to a reification of the state as a central regulator of the urban area in relation to the logic of the functioning of the economy.

Now the state is itself an expression of the totality of contradictory social relationships which must be understood in their movement. The point of departure for an analysis of state intervention cannot be the state itself, still less 'the economy'. A scientific analysis of urban policy must begin with a historical consideration of class relations,

TABLE I *Rate of growth of state expenditure by services and of G.N.P. in France,*
1872–1971 (selected periods)

Coefficient $a \times 10^4$ of log $G = at + b$

	1872–1971	1872–1912	1920–1938	1947–1971	1947–1956	1956–1971
1. Law and order	140	−39	132	220	249	168
2. Defence	132	105	93*	161	503	68
3. Education	223	190	333	457	455	441
4. War veterans	446	–	357	271	559	113
5. Social welfare	280	172	467	449	817	309
6. Transport	146	60*	97*	162	115	242
7. Housing, urbanism	305	31*	115*	15*	299	−78
8. Agriculture	270	174	268	445	1082	185
9. Business, industry	394	235	116*	137	51*	198
10. Miscellaneous	31	−10*	−83	285	618	178
G.N.P.	82	67	71	221	252	224
4 + 5	278	–	382	381	698	245
6 + 7	189	58*	99*	91	207	86
8 + 9	327	183	200*	199	238*	194*
3 + 4 + 5	324	–	359	422	580	348
6 + 7 + 8 + 9	225	72	94*	138	221	138
Total state expenditure	151	44	94	231	379	192

* A non-significant coefficient for a student test $t_{a,v}$ with $a = 0.05$.

Source: C. André, R. Delorme and A. Kouévi, *Etude analytique et numérique des tendences significatives et des facteurs explicatifs de l'évolution des dépenses et recettes publiques françaises au cours de la période 1870–1970*, mimeo (Paris: CEPREMAP, 1974).

class struggle. It must be understood simultaneously as the process of exploitation and resistance to that exploitation, as the dialectical reproduction and transformation of social relations, as class political domination and the alternative power of the dominated classes. This said, the perspective becomes even more complex, because the process of exploitation and domination, resistance to exploitation and class struggle, are realised through a matrix of the totality of the constituent levels of a social formation; that is to say, the dialectic of class struggle is politically condensed in the state, but manifests itself in all domains – in state policies through a series of specific processes: the *accumulation of capital, the development of the productive forces, the reproduction of the labour power, the reproduction of social relations, social struggles, and the internal dynamics of the state apparatus.*

Thus the analytic perspective that we propose is to study 'urban and regional policies' as state interventions in the reproduction of the labour power and in the organisation of space, analysing their multiple determination by the above-mentioned elements. Such a determination is not linear, element by element, but expresses a structural quality: each element determines the others according to a historically given hierarchy and efficacy and it is the totality of these articulations and the dialectic of effects that they provoke which modulates and specifies the interventions of the state. Finally, it is this specific structure of determination which also explains the reciprocal efforts which the process of reproducing the labour force, thus constituted, has on the totality of class relations.

Although the above discussion may appear abstract, it is in fact based on quite precise research operations. Indeed, how do we move forward from the proposed elements? In order to avoid a particular formalism of Marxist theory,[17] we propose to work simultaneously towards the development of conceptual tools, the concrete analysis of historical processes and the discovery of laws structuring the social practices which constitute these processes. To do that it is necessary to analyse and *explain* the formation of the French state's urban policies in a *specified period* (for example, between 1947 and 1975) beginning from the social network composed of the different elements specified above. For purposes of clarity, we have regrouped them in four lines of historical evolution: the evolution of capital; the evolution of production relations; the evolution of social struggles; and the evolution of the state apparatus itself. All exist simultaneously as expressions of class struggle and as 'active reflections' of the totality of these struggles. In addition we are going to consider the evolution of *urban policies of the French state*, characterising them from the point of view of their impact on the totality of class relations.

Finally it will be a question of outlining the existing relations between the principal elements of social evolution which we have noted and the characteristics of urban policies. To better understand this relation we will take account of the variations between different *historical periods* that can be distinguished in the evolution of post-war French society: the period of reconstruction and accumulation (1947–58), the period of monopoly growth at a European level (1958–69), and the

period of economic and political crisis of French capitalism (1968–74)
– which has been exacerbated since 1974.

It is clearly evident that such a study has yet to be done (from the
perspective developed here) and that, besides, it must be a collective
project, which is in progress at this time.[18] We do not possess a sufficient body of research to attempt an explicative synthesis in the
terms just specified. Instead of developing a purely abstract analytic
scheme, we will present some hypotheses on the historical evolution
of urban policies as ways to develop this research perspective.

Capitalist growth in France has gone through three periods since
1945.[19] The first period, between 1947 and 1958 (once the 'restoration
of order' had been established after the Liberation), was characterised not only by the reconstitution of the material basis of production ('the reconstruction') but also by the establishment of the
general conditions of accumulation of capital. This occurred through
systematic state intervention on the means of production
(nationalised industries, transport, energy), on the means of circulation (banks and credit institutions), and as we will see on the reproduction of the labour power. The state becomes central in the
accumulation process, and through it the most important bonds of the
French economy are cemented.

The second period, from 1958 to 1969, was much more than a political
breakpoint. In reality this expresses the movement towards accelerated monopoly accumulation based on three elements: productive
and financial instruments established by the state in the preceeding
period which now generally function favouring large private capital;
European economic integration which qualitatively expands the
market; and the process of concentration of capital sustained and accelerated by the state and the E.E.C., eliminating 'marginal' firms
and 'strengthening' French capitalism. The high level of growth in
this period was accompanied by an accentuation of social disparities
which are not compensated by the state, whose activity is concentrated on aid to private capital accumulation. But this growth produces a triple crisis: economically, because of the decline in the
profitability of capital, relative to the general world level, thus provok-
ing the recession of 1967; socially, with the new blossoming of movements of revolt in 1968; politically, with the abandonment of de
Gaulle, who had become an encumbrance, by the larger French capi-
talists in 1969.

The last period, beginning in 1967–9, was thus a period of crisis:

economic crisis, crisis of social control, crisis of political legitimation. Recession and inflation are articulated in an infernal circle; a level of unemployment above 5 per cent remains for the long term; state economic intervention must choose its priorities; the level of growth reaches its limit.[20] Since 1974 the world economic crisis and the internal political divisions in the dominant classes exacerbate the general crisis of the system, which faces a contradictory double-bind: that of having simultaneously to reinforce exploitation (to re-establish the profit level) and to assure social integration (to re-establish political and ideological hegemony).

The rapidity of capitalist growth, on the basis furnished by the state during the first period, profoundly transformed production relations.[21] The fundamental evolution concerned the massive 'salarisation' of the French population (the wage-earners increased from 62·3 per cent of the working population in 1954 to 81 per cent in 1974).

Those which Nicos Poulantzas calls the 'new petty bourgeoisie' (employees, technicians and salaried staff) experienced a strong growth linked to the diversification of the monopoly capitalist management apparatus and production, while the traditional petty bourgeoisie (artisans, merchants, small industrialists) experienced a sharp drop, due to corporate concentration and modernisation.[22]

Finally, while the working class grew moderately, the peasantry was reduced in size commensurate to the establishment of capitalist agriculture.

It is still necessary to note the development of particular strata within certain classes, for example, the evolution of a larger proportion of immigrants in the working class, and also the growth in the proportion of women in the labour force, particularly as clerical workers. This process continued throughout the three periods, with a particularly strong decline of the traditional petty bourgeoisie between 1954 and 1962 and a sharp expansion in the new petty bourgeoisie between 1968 and 1974. The crisis of 1974 represents a brutal halt in the noted tendency and added two new characteristics to the picture: a high level of structural unemployment; and a reduction in the weight of productive employment relative to non-productive tertiary employment.

Regarding the *social struggles*, after the transitional moment of 1945–7, where the democratic thrust of the liberation created a crisis of bourgeois hegemony which was finally resolved by the political defeat of the working-class movement, there are a number of periods which partially reflect the periodisation of capital accumulation. From 1947 to 1958 there were very important social struggles, particularly by the working class in 1953–4. These were essentially *defensive struggles*, resting on economic demands and protests of principle (foreign policies, for example). The popular defensive struggles, to the extent that they were tough and powerful, led to successful demands, but they were not capable of changing the general policy of the government. Between 1958 and 1967 there was a reversal in the relation of class power: the major political defeat inflicted by Gaullism on the working-class movement and the petty bourgeois republicanism created a situation where the level of mobilisation was attacked. With some exceptions, the total political hegemony of the Right gave them the opportunity to isolate and repress popular struggles. The economic crisis and the exhaustion of charismatic power created a breach in this hegemony through which the movement of May 1968 entered. From this moment there was a shift in trends: from 1967 to 1971 there was a *renewed offensive of social struggles* based on diverse sources of protest, which simultaneously challenged particular situations and the general logic of the system. These developed in France during these years a truly multidimensional social movement: a new workers' movement, student and urban struggles, cultural revolts – all of which were united in their challenge of class domination. This opened a new period, that can be dated from the signing of the Common Programme of the Left (June 1972), from which the offensive of social struggle extended into a general political offensive of the workers' popular movements which provoked, especially since 1974, a profound crisis of political and ideological hegemony for the French bourgeoisie.

The accumulation of capital, the transformation of production relations and the development of social struggles modulate the evolution of the state apparatus. During the Fourth Republic, two distinct changes are observable within the state apparatus: on the one hand, the domination of the Executive by Parliament can be seen as expressing a situation whereby the state apparatus is in the hands of a reigning petty bourgeoisie whose role is to establish a power equilibrium for each major decision; and on the other hand, there is a consolidation of a technocracy of state, relatively detached from parliamentary power, and able to ensure, according to its own criteria, a scale of public accumulation forming the bases of industrialisation and accumulation of the productive apparatus. During the Gaullist phase of the Fifth Republic (1958–69), the internal homogeneity of the state grew. There was a strengthening of executive power at a constitutional level, and at the level of political practices which rested on de Gaulle's charisma. There was also an increasing autonomy of the administration relative to the control of Parliament. This enabled the extraordinary expansion of technocracy whose sense of power was legitimated by the notion of 'public service'. Freed from the hindrance of parliamentary political instability, the state apparatus finally took off in the Gaullist period and became involved in the execution of a series of large projects in the economic domain and foreign policy.

The paradox of this evolution is that the relative autonomy of the state apparatus was used for a mobilisation of resources and public prerogatives for monopoly accumulation. The period 1958–69 was in fact that of the growing concentration of French capital and the insertion of the groups of large enterprises into a multinational network – all this despite considerable social cost, particularly for the petty bourgeoisie and the peasants. To some extent, one can say that the absolute political hegemony of the Right enabled them to impose a state policy entirely favouring the dominant fraction of the power bloc without taking into consideration the interest of other allied fractions, including the supporting classes. It would appear that the Gaullists effectively managed to distance technocracy from instrumental control by the bourgeoisie, while carrying out a policy which strengthened the 'economic power of the French nation', which, given the political and social conditions, could have no meaning other than the re-organisation of French monopoly capital.

The political crisis of 1969 (de Gaulle rejected by the dominant classes because of his attempts to further increase his autonomy and due to the growing inefficacy of his charismatic power) finally transformed the functioning of the role of the French state. Despite the weakness of serious research on this theme, there are some elements available which seem to indicate that even if the centralisation of executive power was maintained,[24] the state's autonomy *vis-à-vis* the direct control of the dominant class was seriously diminished. Tendencies towards the 'privatisation' of public services (the 'true-cost pricing' of public goods in the radio–television reform), the adaptation of the universities to the requirements of business, the introduction of profitability criteria in administrative practice, the Atlantic integration of foreign policies in the lap of the multinational, the opening of nationalised and mixed enterprises to monopoly capital, and so on, are all signs of a general tendency towards destatisation

of the French state and the more direct adaptation of each administration to the capitalist sector which uses its natural outlet.

We have thus witnessed a progressive loss of state autonomy in relation to the dominant class. But this tendency develops in a contradictory way, for if the economic crisis further accelerates this
tendency, because of the requirements of re-establishing the rate of
profit for the monopolies, the crisis of political hegemony (which appeared particularly in 1974 with the political division in the dominant
classes and the push of the Union of the Left) will make the politics of
social integration critical for defusing the growing opposition of the
popular strata. Thus the state will increasingly oscillate between
these functions of aid to monopoly accumulation and political and
ideological legitimation of the bourgeoisie's domination. It is the
Gaullist technocracy which will be the first to succumb to this trend.
Losing its functional autonomy on two levels, it will have to be more
compliant to the large private firms, and also be more attentive to the
repercussions of its intervention. The state apparatus is caught by this
double contradiction: between the requirements of centralisation of
the Executive and the emerging process of 'privatisation' of the Administration; and between the requirements to intensify its accumulation functions and the pressing demands to re-establish its
capacities for legitimation. Such is the crisis of the French state, which
in its historical particularities recalls the similar crises of other capitalist states.[25] But one can deduce from our analysis that this state
crisis is not due to structural economic mechanisms; it is the expression, at the level of the state, of the deterioration of the bourgeoisie's political hegemony, due to the rise of popular struggles and
to the internal cleavages among the fractions of the power bloc.

It is the totality of this historical trajectory which underlies *the evolution of the urban and regional policies of the French state*. It may appear astonishing that there has not been even a superficial historical account
of this historical evolution. It is certainly not a question of fulfilling
this task in a few lines. We only insist on the fundamental *variation* in
the general orientation of the policies in each period in order to
thereby reveal the effects of different sources of social determination
postulated by our hypotheses. First, in the immediate post-war period
(1945–51), the reconstruction of destroyed cities, and above all the
productive apparatus was given priority. The *means of production* were
the principal object of the main state interventions in material equipment. Concerning housing, the 1948 law attempted to stabilise the

level of rent and to prevent the small urban landowners from profiting from the housing crisis to the detriment of social peace, in particular in regard to the wage-earners in the large cities; but this conservative measure was insufficient because, on the contrary, it discouraged private investment in a situation where the state did not control supply. With the accelerated industrialisation, the concentration of the labour force in urban centres, particularly in the Paris region, the housing crisis reached dramatic proportions, hitting the working classes very hard. This situation unleashed extremely strong protests, ranging from illegal housing occupation to national campaigns for social housing between 1947 and 1951. The result was a new urban policy between 1951 and 1963, which *simultaneously emphasised the management of the means of production and the reproduction of the labour power*, particularly in the Paris region. The transportation network was considerably developed, particularly with respect to new industrial locations. But perhaps the most spectacular transformation was the rapid development of a public and para-public sector of social and subsidised housing. The 'Plan Courant' of 1953 enacted a number of measures, the most important of which were: a contribution of 1 per cent total salaries by firms into a special housing fund; the growth of public aid for social housing (the Habitations à Loyers Modérés, or H.L.M.s) through credits and subsidies; the establishment of a very large property developer on the basis of savings drained off by the state – the Société Central Immobilière de la Caisse des Dépôts et Consignations (S.C.I.C.).

Other measures were developed to complete this programme. Some were related to the public control of landed property, as were the Zones à Urbaniser en Priorité (Z.U.P.) and the Zones d'Aménagement Différé (Z.A.D.). Elsewhere public credit measures (especially through the Crédit Foncier) encouraged private home-ownership, especially for one-family dwellings. Housing policies also gave birth to the *grands ensembles*, which were located in the outer suburbs (in order to decrease land costs) and produced according to set standards in the cheapest way possible in order to house as many workers as possible without much regard for quality or amenities. These *grands ensembles*, inhabited by a variety of social groups (workers, employees, lower management), will remain the symbol of an urban policy geared to the fast reproduction of a labour force in order to sustain a labour market and to respond to popular demands. This minimal response to a housing crisis, this socialisation

of cheap housing, in fact led to the deterioration of the day-to-day
social relations, and later to the appearance of new residents' struggles over housing and amenities.[26]

This 'urban social policy' was increasingly challenged during the
second period between 1963 and 1973, which was characterised by an
overriding *preferential aid to monopoly capital*. Thus with regard to the
organisation of the means of production, one can witness an infrastructural planning which reinforced uneven development (and thus
regional imbalance), while at the same time attempted to regulate the
tensions which ensued. The Paris region, whose rapid growth was
accepted and planned in order to create an industrial and tertiary
stronghold able to meet international competition, was given a structure plan which legitimated its growth and proposed new towns to re-
ceive the new influxes of labour. The concept of *metropoles d'equilibre*
attempted to create an urban hierarchy along the same principles of
territorial organisation. The state implemented growth poles for large
French industry, particularly for metallurgy and petrol (Dunkirk and
Fos).

The same absolute priority of aid to capital accumulation was given
to management functions. The policy of new urban centres (La
Défense in Paris, La Part-Dieu in Lyon, etc.) as well as urban renewal
operations[27] correspond largely to the needs of offices and services
required by the reorganisation of the management of a capital in a
period of concentrated growth.

The reproduction of the labour power itself can be understood
through this policy, as a new opportunity for profits. Property development, which has become the prerogative of banks, intervenes in the
markets which state intervention has made profitable. Even the
S.C.I.C. is largely made private and its investments articulated to private capital, which increasingly impose stringent conditions on the
social character of housing.[29] The result was the appearance of new
grands ensembles with greater proportions of middle-class residents.[30]
The provisions of the 1948 law were continually distorted, the
H.L.M.s were made profitable and sharply reduced in numbers, the
property market was entirely taken over by banks, which eventually
led to its collapse.[31] This strategy was reflected in what is known as
the 'Chalandon policy', named after the former Minister of Equipment under President Pompidou: on the one hand, a policy of suburban housing development ensured by a moderate-to-high level of debt
and daily use of the automobile for long-distance commuting; on the

other hand, public assistance for the homeless promoted by the construction of low-quality social housing and the use of 'transit cities' as semi-permanent forms of housing.[32] Such policies also extended to recreational facilities, which on the one hand experienced a reduction in non-profitable collective facilities, and on the other state intervention to manage and make profitable these facilities which favoured market consumption, as in the case of tourism (Operation Languedoc-Rousillon).[33]

At the level of trade, the state favoured the implantation of peripheral supermarkets owned by large commercial chains and created a network of urban motorways necessary for daily life in a city organised in this way. Transport also expressed the structure of movements required by the logic of an urban system directed towards capital accumulation. Thus, for example, the *Réseau Express Regional*, which absorbed the bulk of the budget allocated to collective transport in the Paris region, can only be explained by the need for a massive flow of manual employees required by the concentration of management units in the new directional centres.

In its totality this policy developed a contradiction between the urban apparatus of the state, institutionally, and politically organised around a conception of 'public service', and the consistent practice of systematically favouring private capital accumulation. The famous 'Loi d'orientation foncière' of December 1967, the 'little revolution' of the urbanism of the French state, expressed this contradiction. On the one hand, it gave the state judicial instruments to control urban development by instituting obligatory land-use plans according to criteria of public utility whose provisions could be challenged by third parties. By instituting a 'local amenities tax', it seemed to force private developers to give the communes the funds necessary for collective facilities for the new residents of property developments; but on the other hand, by organising procedures for 'zones of concentrated management' (Z.A.C.) it institutionalised contractual procedures between the state and private capital in order to define the characteristics of each affected housing development. The state used its legal prerogatives to the limit to make possible property development projects beyond the provisions of public controls of urbanisation. Practice has shown that through the procedures of the Z.A.C.s the exception became the rule, and in exchange for insubstantial financial participation the state often put the apparatus of public power at the service of real-estate capital.[34]

The period of crisis which began in 1973–4 was marked by a general change of regional and urban policy, of which the two essential characteristics were: (i) general reduction in public investment; and (ii) emphasis on the *reproduction of social relations*, particularly through initiatives of ideological integration. Urban policies became articulated with the development of the myth of 'the quality of life' – the environment and ecology replaced the 'large national projects' in policy emphasis. This policy was not merely talk. It manifested itself in a painful re-examination of all the large operations undertaken under the Gaullist period: urban renewal was stopped and replaced by institutional rehabilitation of old areas. The projects at Fos and Dunkirk, the tourist development of the coast and so on were cut back; the construction of large residential complexes was stopped; the directional centres were not extended. On the other hand the policy emphasis was on middle-sized cities, the development of green spaces, on less costly intervention which did not greatly disrupt the inherited situations and which allowed 'innovation' at the level of cultural perception of the organisation of life. Actually profiting from the fact that the essential base for the functioning of the urban structure organised around the interests of large capital had been created during the previous period, there was a reinsertion of a growing part of the means of consumption into market relations.

This economic liberalism was accompanied by a flourishing discussion about the quality of life and intervention to create material support for this ideology (for example, action to create green spaces, management of recreational areas, reinforcment of single-family housing, restoration of historic areas). This said, in 1976, the economic crisis marked a sudden halt to the ideological initiatives – which faltered because of their growing disharmony with the economic practices and the regulatory measures of the state apparatus. The move towards a housing policy centred on 'personal assistance' consecrated the failure of social housing and the utilisation of the state to stimulate the market for the benefit of private real-estate promotion. The first-known provisions of the Seventh Plan provide for a quasi-liquidation of public investment in the collective-consumption sector, and this while tenant evictions grew due to non-payment of rent in a period of high unemployment. This is therefore a proof of the hypothesis that urban state intervention does not follow an inevitable progression solely linked to the development of monopoly capital, but that on the contrary there are possible reverses which are a function of class contradictions which underly urban policies.

We have thus moved from an urban and regional state policy centred on the organisation of the means of production and the reproduction of the labour force (first period) to a new policy which favours the accumulation of capital (second period) which provoked such contradictions that there arose an urban policy which attempted to better reproduce social relations (1973–4). But the imperatives of the conjuncture increasingly required that priority once again be given to the objectives of capital accumulation.

This double evolution led to a crisis of French urban policy in 1976 when the majority of the large projects were stopped, when the ideological policies ('quality of life', ecology, middle-sized cities, etc. collapsed, and when the urban planning apparatus failed to adapt to its new task of directing private capital to the cities.

Did this crisis express a crisis of the capitalist state, and if so, through which mediations? For an answer it is necessary to take up the thread of our argument by trying to show the correspondence and disjuncture between the tendencies of social evolution that we have noted and the transformation of the state's urban policies.

During the *first period* capital's first objective was to ensure the means of production and means of reproduction of the labour power without having to make investments, in order to use productive capital directly. The transformation of production relations produced a new stage of proletarianisation which destroyed the pre-existent channels for the reproduction of the labour power and made the new workers dependent upon the general conditions of this reproduction. For their part, social struggles made vociferous economic demands, in particular around the issues of wages, housing, and collective equipment. Finally, the power of the reigning petty bourgeoisie in the state apparatus could not be maintained without a certain satisfaction of the popular economic demands (as well as) a reinforcement of representative mechanisms at the level of local government.

If we now remember the characteristics of urban policy of the period (priority to state intervention in the production of means of production and collective means of consumption), we can observe a convergence and coherence of influence of the four elements of historical evolution towards this effect. The key, however, lies in the relations of power between social classes. The popular classes were in a strong but defensive position, limited to an amelioration of their material living conditions. This forced the dominant classes to give important concession in the collective means of consumption without at all abandoning the priority of public management of the means of production necessary to restore capitalist accumulation.

On the other hand, in the *second period* there appeared a contradiction between the effects produced by the first three factors on urban policy and those determined by the evolution of the state. In effect, the acceleration of monopoly capital accumulation and the development of individual market consumption were consistent with a diversification of the class structure and an expansion of the new petty bourgeoisie which was more sensitive to the ideological aspects of goods and services and to the legislative stratification of consumption. The imposition of these tendencies was easier because the social struggles were generally weak (up to 1968), limited in time and isolated. This explains urban and regional policy entirely dedicated towards the economic and functional interests of the large financial groups. The state which resulted from this evolution, characterised by a large degree of autonomy from the dominant class (even if it tended to serve its interests), led to a strong reduction in local autonomy, neglect of the channels of popular mass integration, and a furtherance of projects designed for large capital of which they frequently did not entirely approve. This sort of 'enlightened despotism' (everything for the bourgeoisie but without the bourgeoisie) of the Gaullist technocracy led to a grandiose urban policy of large national projects which exceeded the capacities for French state intervention, excessively burdened its budget and provoked the hostility of all social classes. This policy failed economically, clearly showing the limits of socialisation of the collective means of production and consumption in a capitalist framework. Besides, it led to a renewal of social struggles, both at a general level (May 1968) and at the level of urban struggles (rise in movements in housing and transportation since 1970). This is fundamental because the main characteristics of this period derive from power relations which were very favourable to the dominant classes.

With regard to the *third period* (of economic and political crisis for French capitalism), there is a new convergence of the four factors towards the urban policy described, centred on the disengagement of the state and the priority of ideological action in order to preserve social relations. From the point of view of capital, the tendency is towards austerity, unemployment, decline of consumption, and, in a certain way, a 'return to Nature', only because life in a forest cottage allows a better absorption of unemployment and enables one to forget the absence of housing in the city. From the point of view of the evolution of production relations, the growing importance of the new petty bourgeoisie increases the role of the dominant ideology urban policy of which it seems to be the privileged recipient. But this permeability of the new salaried strata to the urban theme has a double meaning, for it reinforces their role as an element of popular mobilisation. There is a strong surge of urban struggles which challenge the exclusive privilege accorded to capital and forces the urban technocracy to plan manoeuvres of integration. Finally, the economic disengagement of the state and the maximisation of its ideological function involve a growing 'theatricalisation' of its intervention in the means of consumption, combined with a decollectivisation of socialised consumption: in a way, the less is done, the more it is talked about. The crisis of urban policy can be said to be the crisis of the monopoly capitalist state. This crisis is itself the expression of a progressive reversal in the power relations between classes, which entered a decisive phase in 1974. This reversal in class power relations results from the structural contradictions of advanced capitalism (expressed in the economic crisis and the limits of state intervention) and class struggles which develop at a world level.

What is the effect of this systematic connection between the principal factors in the evolution of French capitalism and the characteristics of state urban intervention?

First, we see that urban and regional policy variation follow a certain logic and that this can perhaps be periodised and made coherent. Thus policies as diverse as housing, transportation, territorial planning, restructuring urban centres, and so on appear objectively articulated as a function of the interest they express at each point. These variations are not arbitrary or linked to this or that particular event. They express the rhythms of capitalist accumulation, class struggle, the evolution of the state. But the social determination of urban policy is not linear: tendencies are often contradictory, and thus state intervention is not separate from, but the result of this totality of contradictions. Thus urban policy is not only a consequence; it acts on social relations, it produces effects on class struggle. More concretely, in contemporary France it sharpens popular struggle, globalises and politicises the opposition to bourgeois hegemony. As an expression of the crisis of the state, it also becomes a key factor in the acceleration of that crisis.

Urban Crisis and Crisis of the State

The characteristic urban crisis of capitalism traditionally appears as a form of capital's incapability, indicated at the beginning of our analysis, to make profitable the means of reproduction of the labour force required both by the process of production and by the demands of the workers. Here it is a question of the contradiction between the objective socialisation of production and consumption and the private appropriation of the management of these two processes. To the extent that the analysis just completed can be supported, one increasingly witnesses a more profound crisis in advanced capitalism: a crisis of urban policy, *a crisis of state intervention on the effects of the urban crisis*. It seems impossible in the 1970s for the capitalist state to continue to assume all those functions in this domain necessary to the reproduction of the system. Let us recall some theoretical elements which can be used to clarify the current trends. State intervention must be understood as starting from variations in the field of class relations, as we have shown in relation to French urban policies. From this point of view the state though *affected by class struggle*, is an apparatus throughout history which results from the crystallisation of the hegemony of successive dominant classes (it is because they are dominant that they hold state power). This apparatus effects a series of functions essential to the reproduction of the existing social order, in a double dialectic in relation to the dominant classes and the dominated classes. We have developed elsewhere[35] a theoretical and empirical analysis of the state apparatus as assuring to the dominant classes the *domination* of their interests and the *regulation* of the contradictions internal to the power bloc or related to the divergent interests of the dominant class. Regarding the dominated classes, the state tries to maximise their *integration* into the order it represents, while maintaining this order through repression. The three periods of urban policy in France represent different state emphases on these different class functions. We moved from *regulation–integration* (first period) to *domination–repression* (second period) to an attempted new combination: *domination–integration*, or the accumulation of capital *and* the reproduction of social relations. It is precisely this combination which led to the crisis of urban policy and the destatisation of intervention in the means of consumption and the failure of integration through ideological manipulation. The combination of *domination–integration* maximised the stability of the power of the dominant class. Its failure is all the more serious because it introduced a fundamental contradiction between the objective socialisation of consumption in monopoly capitalism and the impossibility of its collective management. Thus *the growing intervention of the state in this domain is not ineluctable*, contrary to a number of hypotheses we ourselves, with many others, have put forward in the past. But what is ineluctable is the crisis which this contradiction produces. What is a part of the structural evolution of advanced capitalism is the incapability of capital to make the current society and economy operate without enlarging the functions of the state or without a substantial transformation in the model of accumulation. Why? (1) Partly because of the structural economic contradictions. The tendency for the profit rate to decline has been counteracted during the last thirty years by a series of counter-tendencies (particularly by state intervention) which have unleashed rampant inflation, which increasingly restricts the market and disorganises the process of capital circulation. (2) Partly because of the determination of state policy by the underlying class struggle. The progressive challenge to the power of the bourgeoisie reduces their manoeuvrability and obliges them to intensify state interventions, concentrating them on the essential support of monopoly accumulation.

As the state had constituted an apparatus for the regulation of contradictions in other domains, in particular in the reproduction of the labour force, its abandonment produces veritable convulsions from the point of view of the historical situation. Let us point out that this evolution is not specific to France: it also characterises the developing urban crisis in the United States, where processes of destatisation are having considerable social effect, particularly at the level of local administration.[36] It is there that we have come to the heart of the actual state crisis, which is characterised by the challenge to the apparatus of the interventionist state which developed since the Great Depression of 1929.[37] The socialisation of the costs and the privatisation of profit have structural limits which the monopoly capitalist state has not been able to overcome without producing uncontrollable inflation. The integrative reforms without qualitative transformation of production relations have reached the limit in their capacity to integrate the masses and have been overwhelmed by their consequences. The ideologies of growth and consumption have been replaced by ecological ideologies which do not succeed in legitimating austerity, while objectively they weaken the confidence in two centuries of dynamic capitalist development. The dismantling of urban planning, the disengagement of the state, the poverty of the socialised consumption sector, the abandonment of large projects, the growing disorganisation of the large cities, the corresponding myth of a return to the past (i.e. a 'return to nature') all are diverse traits of a similar phenomenon: the crisis of state intervention on the crisis of the reproduction of the labour force.

Such a crisis is in the process of producing qualitatively important effects on the totality of the class struggle, this for two principal reasons: (i) because the aggravation of contradictions in the domain of socialised consumption affects all the popular strata, not simply the working class; (ii) the diffusion of the urban ideology of the dominant class, treating all social problems as 'urban and spatial', generalises and legitimises these for the petty bourgeois strata. This explains why urban struggles, based on multi-class demands, are in the process of playing a very important role in the mobilisation of the new petty bourgeoisie. This feature is fundamental from the point of view of the strategy of the working-class movement in Western Europe. For a long time the Left has oscillated between social-democratic class collaboration and a Marxist-Leninist ghetto orientated to defending the workers' living conditions. A historical rupture has been in the making for several years. The articulation of new social struggles with alternative democratic politics can lead to a Left-wing electoral victory based on a programme opening the way to socialism. For such a victory to be possible and do not get bogged down in the administrative underground of the bourgeois state, it must not support itself on a coalition of dissatisfactions, but on the political and ideological hegemony of the socialist forces at the mass level. We know that this hegemony must necessarily depend on a transformation of mass consciousness,[38] and that this transformation will not be brought about by televised electoral speeches, but by, and in, struggle.[39] In our historical conditions, the revolutionary's essential task consists above all in *winning the masses*. The battle for the masses replaces the battle of the Winter Palace. What are the prospects?

The working class has a long tradition of struggle and organisation. It is because of that, and at the same time because of its productive role, that it is the fundamental force in a struggle for socialism. But in a strategy of a democratic road towards socialism, one must win *for socialism* (and not only for anti-monopolism) a very large majority of the people. Now our hypothesis is that from the point of view of the objective situation, the new petty bourgeoisie is the class which can most easily rejoin the working class in this offensive against monopoly capitalism. But its ideological transformation depends on its capacity for mobilisation and struggle, and this is seriously handicapped by its lack of tradition and organisation in the sphere of work. On the other hand, in the sphere of socialised consumption, there is a growing homogeneity in the interests of all popular classes, objectively opposed to capitalist logic of production and management of the facilities which form the organisational base of daily life. On this basis, the new petty bourgeoisie mobilises itself more and more, struggles against the urban management of the state, and in this struggle it becomes conscious. In combining social struggles and exemplary democratic management of the cities, hegemony at the mass level and penetration/transformation of the state apparatus, the Left begins to win the battle *for socialism* for the masses beyond the bastions of the working class. Italy, Japan and France have so many experiences which seem to verify in our interpretation. In the large housing complexes of the Paris region, the new petty bourgeoisie votes for the Left significantly more than in other contexts. But this effect does not come from the magical influence of concrete or from a psycho-sociological reaction against 'the quality of life'. In fact, to the extent that life is not a quality but a practice, at the root of this evolution one finds the effect of the socialisation of consumption on the development of mass organisations and of the urban crisis on the burgeoning struggles.[40]

It is in this way that state intervention in the urban crisis produces new popular struggles, which, enlarging the mass base for socialism, themselves deepen the crisis of the capitalist state.

Chapter 4

The Social Function of Urban Planning: State Action in the Urban–Industrial Development of the French Northern Coastline

This chapter aims at analysing the ideological and political background of urban planning on the basis of empirical research which was done on the industrial–urban development in Dunkirk, which has the third largest commercial harbour in France. Dunkirk became a major industrial complex during the 1960s and 1970s because several giant corporations, with the approval of the French government, built the largest steel manufacturing plant in France there as well as oil refineries, ship yards and other industrial factories.

Also, Dunkirk has some of the most radical labour unions in France, and there is a great deal of labour unrest, with almost continuous strikes. Because of this the rapid urban growth that followed the urban development created major social and spatial contradictions which were supposedly problems which could be solved by the planners. This chapter relates what actually happened and is intended to propose a structural explanation from the perspective of a theory of urban planning as a social process.

We provide in Appendix 1 to this chapter (pp. 88–91) some basic data which should make the contradictions we observed much more understandable Appendix 2 to this chapter (p. 92) gives the complete names of the organisations and institutions coded with the French initials in the text.

In fact the research we carried out was much greater in scope, and we have tried to present some understanding of the process of production of the whole urban system. The results of this research are presented in a book which is currently being translated and is to be published by Macmillan: Manuel Castells and Francis Godard, *Monopolville: the Corporations, the State and the Urban Process*.

Planning as a Social Process

The increasing complexity of the urban phenomenon and the acuteness of the problems involved have led to a necessary recourse to institutional mechanisms for the regulation of urban contradictions. Urban planning thus appears as the potential saviour of the crises felt by citizens in their daily lives.

Pressing need and the very high levels of expectations placed upon planning are at the basis of a certain ambiguity as to what is actually understood by urban planning. The question of ambiguity is important, as it can clarify what we are talking about.

One cannot speak of 'planning' in terms of more or less conscious and deliberate action, but only in terms of desired objectives: objectives of regulation, fundamentally determined by their social role, by the institutional place of the intervening agent, especially his membership to an administration which should place him above contradictory social interests and which should enable him to re-adjust the economic and technical problems which are the cause of the urban crisis.

Urban planning, understood as a regulatory action exercised by administrative agencies at different levels and branches of the state, has at its disposal a combination of various means whose examination can provide us with a global perspective on the urban system.

(i) Planning documents which translate planning norms and perspectives – White Papers, S.D.A.U., P.U.D., P.O.S., etc., according to the degree of generality at the level they are found.

(ii) Planning institutions, administrative services, agencies, research, programming and management organisations which are the cogs through which the Administration considers problems.

(iii) Effective interventions upon urban problems carried out by the Administration, whether or not these are made through planning institutions, either according to, or in contradiction with, planning documents, for, and this is an important point, planning 'intervention' should not be confused with planning 'institution'. The problem is to understand not only the reasons for this difference, but also the links which exist between this reality of planning and its presence on organisational charts.

This generally recognised discrepancy is far too often seen in terms of the failures of the objectives and functioning of the planning system.

The planner sees himself as a technician presented with a large number of possibilities which must be continually abandoned in the face of 'social constraints', particularistic demands and budgetary limitations. These always affect his best projects and prevent the great urban developmental tendencies from ever leaving the drawing board. If one were to accept a point of view quite prevalent in the profession, one could say that urban planning serves little purpose at the operational level. Yet planning is expanding everywhere: new institutions multiply, credits are allocated, jobs created, techniques developed, university careers transformed, research undertaken, policies elaborated, and so on. This is the paradox from which we wish to begin: while planning appears unable to regulate urban problems effectively, it is becoming increasingly important as an institution and as a directional instrument of urbanism.

Some may attribute the survival of this paradox to administrative inertia or to the power of the planning profession or planning agencies. But we do not think so, not only because this type of Machiavellian interpretation is based upon an unprovable postulate (man as an individual subject exclusively motivated by personal gain), but also because this hypothesis is contradicted by observation. We are not dealing with an integrated institution, which by sheer inertia resists its own disembodiment, but we are instead witnessing the considerable development of new institutions, at all levels of planning, in all countries, over varying social systems and distinct levels of development. No 'secret society' could ever have been as successful in the universal appropriation of funds and state power! But this realisation makes things more complicated. Assuming that we have rejected an interpretation of planning growth based on a worsening urban crisis, and in addition accept the technical ineffectuality of the planning system as regulator of urban contradictions, we could then suppose that the development of planning institutions is in fact based on a social effectiveness. This in turn could explain the real mechanisms underlying their orientation and organisation.

This is our research objective: to analyse urban planning as a social process, in order to reveal its social effectiveness and relate it to its technical inefficiency, so as to understand the logic of state intervention in urban problems.

Our observation must be very specific since urban growth in this region is exceptional, characterised by its suddenness, and the massiveness of the industrial implantations. Moreover, the concentration of housing and infrastructural provisions, rapid house-building, the pressure of industrial interests on the provision of urban amenities and the total reorganisation of the local administration have led to a complete discontinuity between the provision of productive infrastructures and urban organisation. At the same time our own situation has also been exceptional, as we were able to observe in detail the appearance and transformation of administrative institutions and their planning agencies, as well as the proposal and modification of a number of competing planning schemes.

We have therefore been able to grasp the social process of the creation of planning institutions and elaboration of documents by relating them to the urban problems concerned and to the different administrative interventions used for dealing with them; that is to say, we have used this unusual opportunity for observation to reveal certain mechanisms which are at the basis of the social role of urban planning. These conditions have been so exceptional that these mechanisms cannot be used in the analysis of very different social and urban conditions. Nevertheless, the social logic thus unveiled can be the object of an explanatory proposition (to be verified and completed) which could be applied to situations of intervention other than from those we have observed.

Before beginning our analysis, we must finally say a word about our research method. It consists in identifying the major urban problems of the region and in demonstrating their articulation by establishing a system of urban contradictions specific to that region.

Following this, we have analysed the major aspects of the social and political dynamic underlying the urban system, from the class structure to the transformation of administrative institutions, via the local political scene. Finally, we have examined the planning system in terms of the network of social interests, and administrative organisms and their relationship to the urban problems previously analysed. The analysis was made in terms of the three dimensions already mentioned: regulatory intervention, institutional apparatus, and planning documents. The techniques used include the analysis of documents and statistics, over 120 depth interviews with key informants, participant observation of the work of planning agencies and administrative meetings, and lastly, the use of the Dunkirk urban system itself.

It is from the data that we have collected and studied that we can now analyse urban planning in Dunkirk, and, through it, urban planning as a social process.

A Few Preliminary Reference Points: the Urban System of the Dunkirk Region and the Local Political Scene

Although it is not possible here to provide an exhaustive description of the Dunkirk region, it might be useful to outline a number of aspects which can give some meaning to our analysis of the planning system.[1]

The situation is characterised by the rapid implantation of a massive individual growth pole around a steel-making complex (Usinor–Dunkerque) to which has been added a second steel-making plant (Creusot-Loire), shipyards, a petroleum-processing complex (BP–Total) in addition to a number of existing industrial installations. Still to come and to be directly related to this complex is Vallourec, as are Lesieur and Ciment Lafarge, which are to benefit from the industrial and technical milieu created. The whole of this industrial growth depends upon the construction of an enormous deep-water harbour which will be able to accommodate ships and tankers varying between 125,000 and 500,000 tons. Most of these new infrastructures are being subsidised by the state, and the P.A.D. is to become the sole manager of these gigantic industrial harbour works now under construction.

Such industrial growth not only completely changes the urban landscape, but also entails the influx of a labour force which must be housed, serviced, transported, etc. When one adds to this the multiplicity of services which must be set up for different social categories, one can easily understand the crisis situation in the urban system which we have observed.

To be more precise, we have observed what amounts to a complete blocking in the circuit of production, and in the provision of housing, transport, collective goods and services, as well as in urban centrality and the symbolic elements expressing urban landscape. One important reason for this blocking is the insufficiency of credits in relation to needs. But this is not the most important reason, as the crisis has continued even after the allocation of new resources. The main obstacle is the inadequacy of the traditional circuits of production and provision in relation to the new demands which have been placed upon them. This persistence is not due to a traditionalist 'resistance to change'. It is due to the confrontation of political interests attempting to wrest the control of circuits of production of the urban system as an essential asset against the powerful economic interests which completely dominate the region. What we are witnessing is an effort on the part of the metropolitan government (controlled by locally elected representatives) to retain the control of housing provision in the face of central state strategies to withold credit resources in any networks which could, in an operation as large as the one in Dunkirk, evade state control.

However, this is not to be seen as a direct opposition between the state and the 'locals', but rather as a confrontation of social interests, as a debate between conflictual approaches to urban development. More precisely, the new economy of Dunkirk has profoundly altered the town's social structure, and new interest groups organise the permutation of strategies in the region around their conflicting relations. The old opposition between the harbour bourgeoisie and the traditional working class (dockers, casual labourers, textile workers), which has been mediated by a middle class of provincial notables, is transformed and displaced by the direct opposition between large industrial interests (Usinor, Schneider) which have appropriated the control of the Chamber of Commerce, and the new working class of the large firms which is highly unionised and radical. The diversity of these interests is expressed in terms of the priorities for urban development.
Schematically, one can find the following:

(i) on the one hand, priority attributed to productive equipment and preference given to urban-centre development, with cultural and leisure amenities and residential and leisure zones for management grouped around the old resort of Malo.

(ii) on the other hand, new and old zones of working-class housing (in part structured around the Z.U.P. of the Grande-Synthe, which is virtually a working-class town at the doors of Usinor), construction-yard barracks, hostels for single workers, and rural communes which have now become dormitory towns for the peasants transformed into workers.

Between these two trends one can find a petite bourgeoisie of civil servants, teachers, members of the liberal professions and shopkeepers which is attempting to preserve its social role as guardian of local society. At different times it makes alliances with both of the two principal forces in the locality: sometimes drawing closer to large economic interests in the central city, at other times supporting the popular classes in the working-class suburbs and in the smaller towns of the Dunkirk region.

The diversity of political interests can be seen in the three major political tendencies: the UDR and apolitical controlling the town of Dunkirk itself; socialist notables who have retained predominant positions in most of the older communes; and the Electoral Alliance of the Parties of the Left (Union de Gauche) established upon a trade union base in the new working-class communes. It is the transformed institutional system which mediates and expresses these varying social and political interests. Indeed, the new industrial complex and its accompanying developments have so transformed the spatial scale of daily activities that the responsible administrative institutions have had to be re-adjusted. But this re-adjustment was not based on judicial rules of competence, but according to competing formulae, each of which have attempted to ensure the primacy of the social interests mentioned above. For this, the socialist notables set up the first voluntary metropolitan government in France, granting it maximum jurisdiction. They thus have made it a key instrument in their attempt to counterbalance the 'industrial power' of the economic groups with that of the 'urban power' of local institutions.

The state, faced with an institutional set-up which could threaten the smooth implementation of a economic project of international scale, at one point envisaged the formula of an inter-ministerial mission which would be in charge of urban planning, as had been done in Fos. But in the face of the complexity and the relative strength of local society, the option taken was to support the town of Dunkirk, which was socially and politically in favour of a narrow collaboration with the large firms. This was done by a progressive strengthening of the town's position by means of a carefully calculated fusion of communes. This was the project of the *Grand Dunkerque*, which has already begun with the amalgamation of Dunkirk with Malo-les-bains, then Rosendäel, and then Petite-Synthe, which has increased the population of Dunkirk from 27,000 inhabitants in 1968 to 80,000 in 1972 and a total of 150,000 inhabitants for the conurbation as a whole.

This impetus on the part of the most powerful classes has met the resistance of the 'opposition' through the strengthening of the metropolitan government. The latter can maintain control by means of an alliance between socialist notables and the Electoral Alliance of Left

Parties, which in political terms reflects the alliance between the traditional petite bourgeoisie and various working-class strata. This situation influences the planning process to the extent that *ad hoc* organisms expressing conflicting social interests can at various times be inserted into the administrative institutions.

The Apparent Failure of Urban Planning in Dunkirk

As soon as the large industrial and harbour works had been started, the working-class estate of Grande-Synthe was built, and new housing projects became inevitable necessities, planning institutions were set up and plans were elaborated. At first the Chamber of Commerce and Industry set up a research bureau which became the basis of a planning agency (AGUR) for the metropolitan government and which received the support of the Minister of Equipment. A first planning document, entitled *Livre Blanc: Dunkerque 2000*, was produced by this agency.

Meanwhile, OREAM-Nord prepared within the framework of its general structure plan for the North and the Pas-de-Calais, a S.D.A.U. for the coastal region. Finally, just at the point when new urban implantations were to be accelerated, AGUR: also prepared a S.D.A.U. of the Dunkirk region, which, coinciding with the strengthening of the metropolitan government aimed, according to different versions, at the coherent and operational ordering of the totality of urban growth.

Now, what is initially striking is the absence of any relationship between plans and planning institutions on the one hand, and the options actually adopted in the physical planning of Dunkirk on the other. Thus industrial planning has been on the one hand the entire responsibility of the Port Authority, while on the other the D.D.E. has been responsible for the network of roads. AGUR can only ratify options taken in the first instance and express preferences in the second. This is already a fundamental aspect of the weak hold which planners have on urban development, for it is largely the organisation of productive infrastructures (which has been made according to a completely autonomous logic linked to the industrial growth-pole project) which determines the whole of the urban system.

Still, one could argue that the planner's role is to adapt 'the city' to the imperatives of growth. But concrete analysis shows that this is not the case. In fact, the majority of future housing programmes (which would double the Z.U.P. of Grande-Synthe and create a new one at Gravelines amounting to over 5000 new dwellings), have been prepared outside the S.D.A.U. and later integrated within it due to the pressures exerted by the Metropolitan government.

The amenities provided by the town of Dunkirk, particularly for sports and leisure, were made without preliminary consultation with AGUR which was seen as suspect by virtue of its membership in the metropolitan government. Planners do not even act upon the blocking of public transport, namely its non-extension on the periphery of the conurbation where it would impinge upon a private transport company serving working-class suburbs. Finally, the establishment of a hierarchy of urban centres in the conurbation was fixed through negotiation with Dunkirk and the Chamber of Commerce, and was later ratified by the S.D.A.U. Neither the office of the H.L.M., under the control of the metropolitan government nor the Société d'Equipement du Nord altered their programmes according to the forecasts of planners. Moreover, the coastal structure plan project, with the creation of the Syndicat d'Etudes Mixtes Calais–Dunkerque, did not even consider it necessary to have representatives of the urban planning agencies among its members.

Finally, and more importantly, the S.D.A.U. of Dunkirk was completed only in 1972, when most of the more important industrial and urban options had already been taken and their projects started (including financing), all this obviously without any significant participation on the part of the planners in decision-making.

It would appear therefore that urban planning has had no role to play in the transformation of Dunkirk, and that planners are once more experts which have been left out due to the pressures of immediate economic and political interests. Yet, not only has there been a proliferation of planning organisms and a great production of planning documents, but we have also witnessed a fierce battle between social interests and different administrations for the control of planning institutions in an attempt to impose upon them the various approved schemes.

We thus return to the paradox we had elaborated above, and in order to make some general conclusions we must examine its social logic in the case of Dunkirk.

The Battle of the Planning Documents: Social Interests, Spatial Models and Debates on the City

If planning has a weak technical function, and if it nevertheless continues to grow despite this, it is because it has in fact a precise social function which is very closely linked to the social and political interests underlying urban power relations.

In order to verify such a statement and to determine the specific function it has in relation to the interplay of interests, one only needs to read planning documents and to follow their evolution and debates, not in the light of planning norms but in the essentially shifting conjuncture of urban politics.

Thus the first planning document of the new Dunkirk, *Livre Blanc: Dunkerque 2000*, prepared by the Chamber of Commerce, AGUR, the *communauté urbaine* and the Ministry of Equipment, and approved by the Town Hall of Dunkirk, has as foremost objective the strengthening of the town of Dunkirk in order to ensure a centrality necessary for industrial development and the attraction of key personnel essential for an urban milieu. Therefore its most emphasised goals are related to commercial and leisure amenities in the city centre, the others being diverse and broad. This document, produced in 1968, represents the last moment of consensus between the old bourgeoisie of Dunkirk (the commercial and maritime bourgeoisie, and the local notables) who then proposed an urban milieu as a complement to the developing industrial milieu – thus the ode to the 'noble functions' of the city and the insistence upon centrality, without, however, considering all the new problems which were arising following the influx of labour. This largely explains its unanimous approval and its immediate obsolescence. As soon as stakes become more definite and forces reorganised, the same planning agency adopted very different objectives for its S.D.A.U., arousing parallel reactions on the part of large industrial interests which are mostly expressed by the coastal structure plan put forward by the OREAM-Nord.

The turning point was 1971. The March municipal elections heralded strong gains for the Electoral Alliance of Left Parties, notably in Grande-Synthe ('Usinor City'), whose new mayor, a worker at Usinor, was a member of the Parti Socialiste and the C.F.D.T. union. Meanwhile, the mayor of Dunkirk, supported by the U.D.R., made a triumphant return. The *communauté urbaine* stayed Left, and the *commission d'urbanisme*, to which AGUR is related, was to be presided over by the new mayor of Grande-Synthe. In the meantime Usinor assumed the presidency of the Chamber of Commerce and Industry, thus displacing the last vestiges of the local bourgeoisie.

The S.D.A.U. published in 1971 could not arouse even minimal consensus, and came out as a generalist and provisional document. Finally, the radical tendency of the metropolitan government was able to impose itself and make the S.D.A.U. its own manifesto. The option adopted is the development of the working-class estate and the construction of others, but this time adding amenities, open spaces, leisure centres, etc.

The document also preached a more diversified renewal of industrial growth, with plans for a new industrial estate for light industry – this in contradiction with the projects of large enterprises who wanted an extremely specialised pole of heavy industry.

In other words, AGUR's new S.D.A.U. expresses the new influence of the unions in the metropolitan government, an influence aimed at obtaining on the one hand more equipment and amenities, and on the other a wider and more diversified labour market which could integrate female employment.

But this S.D.A.U. is constrained by the fact that it is also that of the metropolitan government, which as an administrative institution cannot entirely oppose the general economic objectives of the state, which are also those of the large enterprises. The document must account for the urban requirements of the various groups concerned. Thus in the S.D.A.U., the town of Dunkirk will have its tertiary provisions (administrative, commercial and leisure) and its urban-renewal programmes; large enterprises and the harbour will keep their industrial zones and the roads network necessary for exchange and the draining of the rural labour reserve; the production and provision of housing, centralised by the presidency of the *communauté urbaine* will have some strategies related to the concentration of certain communes and others to their preservation; each peripheral burgh is given an important dose of amenities – managers can have their residential and leisure zones, workers can have more amenities, farmers can keep their agricultural lands now preserved in green belts for the city dwellers. The whole is then linked up by a network of roads which will ensure the coherence of the proposed urban system. All that needs to be done is its financing! One can only guess that everything must be done according to priorities and stages, but on these points the S.D.A.U. is vague. Nevertheless, the various interests are respected and the coherence of the whole preserved.

In contrast, the littoral structure plan proposed by OREAM-Nord and supported by central state is not so considerate. Its goals are clear-cut and almost exclusively in accordance with those interests at the basis of the development of the large steel complex of international scale.

This scheme can thus propose a coastal motorway useful for industry, but this divides the urban centre in two; provisions are made for an industrial polluting corridor, whereas AGUR's S.D.A.U. planned for a wooded 'green lung' for the working-class estates to the west.

What becomes apparent is that the OREAM scheme has only a few similarities with the AGUR one. These are: the development of leisure amenities to the East and a tourist leisure zone to the south around les Bergues; the preservation of green belt in the plains; and the conservation of the urban harbours at Gravelines, Grand and Petit Port Phillippe. However, with everything concerning urban planning proper, the two schemes are in direct opposition with each other.

OREAM insists on the creation of a vast metropolitan area (within the Calais–St Omer–Dunkirk triangle) accompanied by the development of a number of new urban poles, while AGUR is interested in the development of the Dunkirk town centre, which is seen as the focus for a conglomeration of between 180,000 and 250,000 inhabitants. OREAM is proposing urbanisation running parallel to the coast, to the limits of the landward hills, and in the immediate future it envisages the creation of residential zones to the east of Dunkirk, while AGUR proposes a high-density concentric development scheme beginning from the crown of Dunkirk and extending itself according to a North–South or North–South–West axis, around the leisure zones of Bergues and Cappelle, thus strengthening the urban core. OREAM designates the entire west coastal zone for industrialisation, while AGUR wishes to preserve and extend the working-class estates, surrounding them with open spaces. Whereas OREAM anticipates the dispersion of administrative and university centres between Calais–St Omer–Dunkirk, AGUR hopes to see Dunkirk become an important administrative and university centre for the whole coast.

The social logic of these oppositions is fairly clear: for OREAM Dunkirk is a productive unit which can be understood only in terms of technical and industrial planning for the northern region, which is itself one of the major strategies of the plan. First and foremost, according to the requirements of the large enterprises, urban planning for Dunkirk is simply a technical issue. For AGUR, which is firmly based in the local political scene, other realities are more compelling; AGUR's planning proposals must satisfy certain local requirements, but these are within a framework which does not allow it any decision-making powers.

Whatever the case, one is witnessing a debate on the city which attempts to make coherent the requirements of urban organisation. These are in turn determined by dominant social interests inside administrative institutions from which planning agencies arise.

The Creation and Transformation of Planning Agencies: Technical Requirements or Socio-political Conflicts

The fact that planning documents are only pronouncements does not make them less important, for it is important in a situation so fluid and charged with economic and political interests to be able to speak and to speak well, to present one's own interests and to encompass rationally all others. But there is more in the extra-technical intervention of urban planning. The usefulness of planning agencies as positions within administrations used to make known particular options is demonstrated by the bitterness of the political and institutional battles between various groups for the control of these institutions.

Moreover, a concrete analysis, such as the one done on Dunkirk, shows that social conflicts reproduce at the level of institutions the very oppositions which underline the ideological oppositions expressed by the planning documents.

It is important to understand, however, that the conflicts at the basis of competing formula in institutions and planning agencies are not merely inevitable quarrels between groups or individuals attempting to maximise their gains. These conflicts arise and develop from the structural contradictions between social interests and the requirements thus determined with regard to urban organisation. Therefore in Dunkirk one can only understand this veritable 'lions' den' by starting from an analysis of the structurally determined interests of social forces (large firms and central administration; the working-class; old and new middle classes), as well as their ·political expression and the transcription of this set of interests upon the specific sphere of urban problems.

It is by keeping in mind this contradictary structure of social interests that we can better understand those institutional strategies centred upon the production and control of planning organisms. The richness and significance of the process observed merits more attention.

The first planning organism of Dunkirk was the *'comité dunkerquois d'études économiques et sociales* (C.D.E.E.S.), set up in 1955 by the Chamber of Commerce and Industry. The C.D.E.E.S. which was well integrated with such regional organisms as the *comité regional d'expansion* had an advisory role between 1955 and 1968. It was in 1967, during a seminar (the Monts des Cats seminar), that representatives from the state, professional associations and local authorities were brought together and that C.D.E.E.S. put itself forward as an advisory body to undertake the co-ordination of those concerned in the local political scene. The publication of the Land Act towards the end of 1967, and the obligation it laid upon all towns with over 100,000 inhabitants to set up a planning organism, led the C.D.E.E.S. to clarify further its intentions of becoming the planning agency and preparing the S.D.A.U.

The Mayor of Dunkirk supports this proposal, which can provide the local bourgeoisie, and especially the harbour bourgeoisie with an opportunity to re-enforce its functions of 'domination–regulation–integration' of the local institutional system.

However, 1968 was the year that the *communauté urbaine* was set up due to the impetus of the socialist deputy. This faction of the petty bourgeoisie believed it was doing well by the creation in the interim of a *communauté urbaine*, a planning agency. For its part, the G.E.P. of the north curbed the impulsiveness of the C.D.E.E.S's control over planning projects. The agency was finally created in May 1968 and located in the town hall. The setting up of the planning agency was made in close liaison with the C.D.E.E.S., which eventually accepted this mixed formula as a reasonable compromise. When the *communauté urbaine*, through the intermediary of its vice-president assumed the presidency of the planning agency, it found it functioning organically with the C.D.E.E.S.

AGUR, half-financed by the metropolitan government and half by the M.E.L., does not operate according to the intentions of the President of the *communauté urbaine* as an agency of the *communauté*, but rather as one of the town of Dunkirk and of the C.C.I.D. (as is evident by the *Livre Blanc*). This would explain the defiance of the President of the *communauté urbaine vis-à-vis* AGUR, as well as the restrictions upon the services provided by the M.E.L. (e.g. refusal of building permits), in order to 'restore these Utopians to reason'.

Great State Strategies and Conflicts Internal to the Administration

The eviction from controlling positions in the C.C.I.D. and C.D.E.E.S. of the dominant fraction of the harbour bourgeoisie by the large firms led to the dissolution of the C.D.E.E.S. in 1971 and to the weakening of AGUR, thus enabling the promotion of a central inter-ministerial mission which could undertake the entire development of the Calais–Dunkirk coastline.

This mission, prepared by DATAR, was to enable central adminis-tration, in liaison with the plan prepared with OREAM, to submit local interests to the logic of the development of large monopoly in-dustry. It would, moreover, enable the Association du Grand Dun-kerque to make some gains over the metropolitan government with a view to reducing the latter's role.

The project for such a mission failed primarily because it met oppo-sition by certain branches inside the central administration, for example those of the M.E.L. and the Prefecture who had prepared their own administrative formulae through the integration of local in-stitutions for the control of planning operations on the coast.

The M.E.L. has its own local facilities for setting up networks of roads (the Ponts et Chausées), and with the D.D.E. controls local infrastructural policies; it also has technicians with AGUR. For his part, the Prefect of the Northern region has under his aegis the Groupe d'Industrialisation de Dunkerque, which includes all the executive technicians involved in the development of the region. Tech-nicians with the metropolitan government have regular contacts with the Prefecture and good technical relations. Moreover, during the visit of Jérôme Monod (*Délégué Général à l'Aménagement du Térritoire et à l'Action Régionale*) to Gravelines in July 1970, the amalgamation of Calais and Dunkirk was proposed. The Prefect had then suggested the creation of a *Syndicat d'Etudes Mixte* comprising representatives from the C.C.I, the harbour and local authorities which were to be under the aegis of a co-ordinator appointed by him, a technician from the Direction Departementale de l'Equipement.

The announcement of an inter-ministerial mission was to stimulate the setting up of the syndicate. While the mission was to function according to domination and regulation, the syndicate proposed integration and regulation. This second formula represented a co-ordinating operation which would reduce the risks of opposition by all local technical and political institutions, as well as the radicalisation and strengthening of Left political movements.

The *Syndicat d'Etudes Mixte* was set up, after a series of hard negotiations in March 1972. It represented scope for manoeuvrability which became all the more important when in March 1971 Calais elected a Communist mayor to an Electoral Alliance of the Left municipality, and Dunkirk itself experienced Left-wing gains. Originally the *Syndicat d'Etudes Mixte* was conceived as a planning and co-ordinating body operating at three levels:

(i) as consultative and co-ordinating body for employers;

(ii) as inter-communal body for Dunkirk and Calais; and

(iii) as planning agency for the littoral based on AGUR and ORETUR (planning agency for Calais).

The responsibilities of the Prefect's mission were to engage in negotiations, and to ensure the coherence of all coastal planning, with the assistance of the two Directeurs Departementaux de l'Equipement and the director of the Port Autonome, with the support of the two départements. The *chargé de mission*, who was backed up by OREAM, was appointed deputy to the D.D.E. of the North and the Pas-de-Calais in September 1971, thus administratively linking up the coastal parts of the two départements.

The announcement by the Prefect of the Syndicat d'Etudes Mixte provoked a veritable thunderbolt in the already troubled skies of Dunkirk. The swift setting-up of the syndicate bore no relationship to the urban stakes of the time. The coastal industrial development, especially between Gravelines and Calais, was not due before 1980–85. The speed by which the institutional and planning systems were set up is really related to the acquisition of control of development options within a specific class perspective.

Meanwhile there was also a race for the publication and administration of planning schemes and structure plans, because while for some the aim was to hasten the implementation of the S.D.A.U., for others it was to deflect or block it. However, this institutional race had begun when already certain irreversible decisions had been taken with regards to the Dunkirk urban core.

The Establishment of the Syndicat d'Etudes Mixte and the Reaction of Local Authorities

The establishment of the *Syndicat d'Etudes Mixte* took place at several levels. For the employers this was fairly straightforward since a liaison committee grouping together the C.C.I. of Dunkirk–Calais–St Omer and Boulogne already existed (since 1970), in addition to a co-ordinating committee for the ports of Calais and Dunkirk associating the C.C.I.D–C.C.I.C. and P.A.D. set up in March 1971.

But since the establishment of the syndicate, the C.C.I. of Calais was represented by its president, while that of Dunkirk by its vice-president only, i.e. by the one who used to preside over the C.C.I.D. when it was still representing the interests of the harbour bourgeoisie. This would suggest that medium-sized firms were present and ready to participate actively in the SECADU. Their common interest effec-tively resided in industrial development on the coast-line, in order to avoid the blocking of development around a single steel industry, and to promote at the same time a training scheme in view of the implanta-tion of medium and diversified industries.

For their part, large employers, after their failure to have a central-ised mission, set up the 'coastal industrialisation group' in order to counter the syndicate. This group, the initiative or the Association pour l'Expansion Industrial (APEX), had as president the commis-sioner for industrial reconversion who was also *chargé de mission* to DATAR. He therefore had direct links with central urban planning and with the interministerial group in charge of monitoring the development of the Calais–Dunkirk coastline.

The most important monopolies were represented by this group and it was in close contact with the highest political levels. Its first ob-jective was to ensure industrial infrastructural provision for the steel and metal monopolies, according to the plan put forward by them when the Dunkirk site was reserved for the steel industry.

It was imperative for the large monopolies and DATAR to act as quickly as possible in setting up industrial provisions, as it was in their best interest to intervene in the urban planning of the coastline. How-ever, they were equally quickly countered by the local political insti-tutions grouped around the metropolitan governments of Dunkirk and Calais. The rapid intervention of the latter had been possible as a result of a political agreement between the two conglomerations, which had been strengthened by a strong current of political union between communist and socialist parties at the time. It was under such an impetus that the intercommunal syndicate took over the leadership of the SECADU in March 1971.

A reading of the SECADU statute reveal a number of divergences from the Prefect's initial projects. In fact, not only do the local authorities take over SECADU and resolve to initiate and co-ordinate all schemes on the Calais–Dunkirk coast, but also constitute themselves as the only body responsible to departmental, regional and national authorities. This put into question the co-ordinating role of the Dunkirk 'prefecture', as SECADU affirmed the duty and power to fulfill it. The constitution of SECADU is important as it signalled a turning-point in November 1971 in central administration's regional policy.

Prefect Dupuch, having already proven himself in the industrial restructuration in Lorraine, replaced Prefect Dumont. His job was to prepare the long-term bases upon which the administration could intervene more directly, and to limit in the short term the electoral damages at the legislative elections of March 1973 which could jeopardise the industrial reconversion of the North. Prefect Dupuch's approach was not the same as that of his predecessor; he preferred direct action to co-ordination, and exercised a much firmer diplomacy with the local authorities.

While the 'co-ordinating' prefect lost his prefectoral support and was caught in an inextricable interplay of contradictions and was finally made powerless by SECADU, SECADU itself was deprived of the support of the Ministry of Equipment and as such of the technical and financial resources necessary for its important projects.

Some doubts now exist as to who will be in charge of infrastructural provisions. What is meant by them? Do they include transport networks? Who will finance them? This last question was in fact posed by the president of the metropolitan government himself during the founding meeting of SECADU. Finally, once again, the central administration (Prefect Ministry and DATAR) must wait for the local political institutions.

With regards to the first two questions, one can put forward the following hypothesis: SECADU, through the co-ordination of projects concerning the whole of industrial and transport planning, could attempt to control the whole planning process, housing as well as certain other indispensable social needs. It could by its own means ensure the financing of housing, and by exercising strong institutional and political pressure, and (in the political conjuncture, the hypothesis cannot be excluded) obtain the financing of the collective goods for the region. This leaves unanswered the question of the network of roads, which will not fail to create new enlarged urban contradictions given that they are in close interaction with the location of residential zones (the latter being controlled by SECADU).

The actual planning organisms were not invited at the constitution of SECADU, which would indicate political will on the part of the organisers for a better local control of planning schemes. Here again one can observe a race for the control of planning schemes for the Calais–Dunkirk coast.

OREAM was due for dissolution once its S.D.A.U. had been prepared, but at one point it attempted to recycle itself by taking advantage of the opposition between the president of the metropolitan government and AGUR, and the coastal planning projects which had been put forward following the visit of Jérôme Monod to Gravelines in July 1970. It credited itself with having initiated the collaboration between Calais and Dunkirk by having invited the *Déléqué Général à l'Aménagement du Térritoire et à L'Action Régionale* (on which OREAM depends) along with representatives of the two towns, and had also attempted to arrogate the power to co-ordinate the development of the littoral as an extension of DATAR.

This first attempt having failed (OREAM had to drag its S.D.A.U. to Dunkirk), OREAM, which had been dissolved in Lille, recycled a few of its members which were then representing DATAR into a group formed during 1971 by the 'co-ordinator' prefect, which called itself the *Groupe de liaison d'amenagement sur le littoral*. A question to ask is whether DATAR would not in fact have preferred to leave the more technical work of elaborating schemes for the P.O.S. to the local agencies. But this strategy appeared to be the more difficult since the 'co-ordinator' prefect saw his powers reduced and local political institutions decided to give themselves the means of controlling planning operations.

The disagreement between AGUR and the president of the metropolitan government during its creation (while it was functioning in conjunction with the C.D.E.E.S:) had led him to envisage solutions in terms of a fusion between AGUR and ORETUR complemented with outside technicians. AGUR's change of outlook (the motives of which have been exposed) and its assertion of an ideology of local power with strong Gamiste reminiscences (GAM = Groupes d'Actions Municipaux) which were helped by the eviction of the C.D.E.E.S. led the metropolitan government to give AGUR new means of becoming (with ORETUR) the planning agency for the coast.

The reconstitution of AGUR gave it new powers to elaborate the coastal structure plan and to co-ordinate schemes. This new Agence d'Urbanisme de la région de Dunkerque was administered under the law of 1 July 1901. It was financed by state subsidies, subsidies by the metropolitan government and the Department, membership fees, contracts for projects, loans, giving to the planning agency much greater financial autonomy than before. The personalities which it wanted to include in its various organs (Prefect, D.D.E., T.P.G., mayors of the S.D.A.U.s, director of the G.E.P., director to the technical services of the metropolitan government of the P.A.D. and the C.C.I.D, etc.) meant that it could become a unique co-ordinating organism for littoral projects. Its increase in membership (eleven members in 1968, twenty-nine members in 1972, and a forecast of sixty members) confirms its intention of becoming in the short or long term the littoral planning agency. AGUR had the immense advantage over ORETUR of being able to rely on local political institutions. In this way ORETUR saw its S.D.A.U. for Calais refused after Left-wing municipal gains in 1971. This particular S.D.A.U. clearly revealed ORETUR's orientation, which was to restructure the Calais town centre according to the needs of the firms in Calais.

The establishment of a coastal planning agency based on AGUR will enable local institutions in Dunkirk to ensure infrastructural and urban planning projects in the Calais–Dunkirk complex without having to call upon ORETUR, whose links with the Chamber of Commerce and Industry means that it now resembles the old AGUR which the president of the metropolitan government had not wanted.

This established, it becomes clear that in such a decanted situation, two organisms remain to ensure basically the same functions: on the one hand, the coastal agency we have just mentioned; and on the other, the Group *de liason de l'amenagement sur le littoral*. Two organisms being one too many; conflicts could only start anew, this time with the difference that, unlike the first period, they would be institutionally clearer and more direct.

Urban Planning as Ideological Discourse and Negotiating Instrument

We are now in a position to understand at one and the same time the *raison d'être* and opposing motives of the various urban interest groups, as well as the actual role played by urban planning in the urbanisation process of the Dunkirk coast. In fact, it we attempt to synthesise our analyses so far, we can retrace the wider tendencies characterising urban planning on the Dunkirk coast.

The opposition between the scheme presented by OREAM and that presented by AGUR expresses the confrontation between a conception of Dunkirk as being solely a unit of production inside a much greater whole, and one whereby the growth of the pole could give it a greater political autonomy for the benefit of one or other of the local elites who hold key positions in the institutional system. At the institutional level, this opposition corresponds on the one hand to the inter-ministerial missions, and on the other to local authorities' planning institutions.

One knows that this institutional conflict was settled by an unstable compromise exercised through the formula of the *Syndicat d'Etudes Mixte* and the flexible role of the 'co-ordinator' for planning with local programming antennae. Can one say the same for urban plans? It would seem not, for the approved scheme differs considerably from OREAM's first proposal. Would this mean that the 'locals' have won? In reality things are more complicated. The approved S.D.A.U. only gives an apparent coherence to the three main currents present in the local political scene, which are, as we already know, linked to specific interests:

(i) Dunkirk sees its projects as aimed at reinforcing the symbols of urban centrality, of providing housing and amenities for management – in a word, everything must contribute to its prestige;

(ii) the metropolitan government ratifies all its problems of equipment and housing, in particular that of the increasing density of the working-class communes to the West – the lay-out of the roads follows the internal logic of the communes' territory;

(iii) within the metropolitan government the growing trend towards the defence of the immediate interests of the resident population means that large gains have been made to obtain better and more decentralised amenities, leisure facilities and open spaces.

It would now appear that everyone is satisfied. All that needs to be done is to finance and plan the whole. The S.D.A.U. declares a cease-fire on paper by ratifying these preferences. But this beautiful coherence only concerns the Dunkirk conglomeration itself – the only domain recognised as falling under the jurisdiction of the metropolitan government.

Yet the S.D.A.U. may still provoke new contradictions where the provision of new industrial zones is concerned, particularly the one bordering on the canal which had engendered very hostile reactions. This project effectively goes against the interests of not only large plants already located, but also against that of state growth-threshold strategies, and against central administration, which is already overwhelmed by the contradictions arising out of current levels of industrial concentration.

On the other hand, industrial growth which escapes the control of the P.A.D. means the presence of diverse economic groups and the strengthening of political forces controlling local institutions. This is why the balance attained at the level of urban planning is called into question by a new industrialisation project whose declaration of intentions is made through proposals for spatial planning.

This last sequence of events shows the role played by urban planning in the urbanisation of the Dunkirk coast with even greater clarity. We have been able to observe that the purely technical operations were in fact secondary in relation to the establishment of the large planning orientations. We could even add that what is truly operational in reality falls under the competence of the various administrations concerned with the management of urban problems: the D.D.E. for transport, the S.E.D.N. and H.L.M. for housing, equipment and facilities, and so on.

One is of course left with the issue of projects, data collection and use, analyses of social and economic trends, but there is agreement in distinguishing between a planning agency and a planning consultancy. This distinction is more justified by the socio-political role of planning agencies than by their technical regulation function, for, as we have also seen, this regulation consists essentially of prompt intervention, responding to its own logic according to the place it has in the economic process as a whole.

But what is the socio-political role of urban planning? Is it a vast enterprise of ideological mystification? Our results would dismiss such a simplistic view, and introduce instead an interpretation of the planning process as being the means whereby two objectives can be realised:

(1) *Urban planning is a statement on the city which follows the logic of an urban organisation according to different social interests. In extreme cases, when planning agencies must submit completely to a dominant social and political force, this statement becomes one of rationalisation of coherent interests.*

On the other hand, another type of planning pronouncement can be identified from planning schemes: that of harmony and agreement of contradictory demands, rubbing out these contradictions by colouring them differently on a map, or more seriously by separating them spatially (zoning), or temporally (phased development), thus enabling divergent or even contradictory social demands to be represented in the same scheme.

Thus planning schemes appear as scenarios for compromise, inside of course a dominance of structural interests which are never called into question. For example, one would never consider depriving Usinor of a functional network of roads, or consider building H.L.M.s on the resort beaches.

Consequently, what appears significant in our analysis is less the declarational value of plans than their specification of the contents to be declared. In reality they are not so much the rationalisations of a dominant ideology than elements for integration and conciliation, outlining the compatibility of a set of decisions which escapes them in order to show the possibility, even the necessity, of peaceful coexistance.

(2) *As an urban political process, planning effectively appears to be a 'place' for negotiations and mediated expressions of the conflicts and tendencies which (according to general social determinations) confront urban organisations, and through it the whole of social and economic organisations.*

We do not mean by 'place' of negotiation that planning institutions are the passive vessels for various pressure groups, but that instead we consider them as a privileged means of expressing oppositions and conflicts, and by these the possibilities of bargaining, accommodation and compromise, for which purpose the *master plan* will later serve.

The role of the planner is much more that of an intermediary than that of a technician. To be more precise, he uses the prestige of neutrality and technical competence to present himself as a professional and 'scientist' above conflict, and as such is in a comfortable position to arbitrate between the various social partners. In this way he can carry out the interests of the central administration in a much more efficient manner than he would were he to present himself as the ideological mouthpiece of the dominant faction. It is in this way that planning is part of the process of social regulation, rather than that of direct domination on the part of the class in power.

In recognising that in the case of Dunkirk, planning is a process of social negotiation between conflictual urban interests, one comes close to a number of classical sociological hypotheses and observations on planning and planners in particular. But it is not enough simply to describe a mechanism which is increasingly becoming characteristic of all planning insitutions in advanced capitalist countries; one must also show what is the stake to be negotiated, how the roles of that process were determined and, especially why urban planning is fundamentally a means of negotiation in urban politics rather than the conscious controller of growth.

We must add, however, an important note: agreement and compromise are possible precisely because they are made between reconcilable interests; but if planning is indeed a process of negotiation this does not mean that all is negotiable. One is only negotiating those themes and options which in a given historical conjuncture do not fundamentally contradict structurally dominant interests. More precisely, this means that this negotiation process concerns only those different factions of the dominant classes and the interests of the dominated classes as such, i.e. only within the limits defined by the structural laws of the dominant mode of production. Such a situation is not due to the intrinsically perverse nature of urban planning, but simply to its insertion inside the central administration's mechanism and consequently to its submission to the social laws which govern it, which we have not only denounced but also verified in the concrete functioning of the central administration in Dunkirk.

Does this mean that the interests specific to the dominated classes have no chance of expressing themselves at the level of urban planning? That it cannot exert any influence? Absolutely not. Our analysis is the proof, for we have seen the fundamental role played by the last S.D.A.U. of Dunkirk as a result of the growth of the Electoral Alliance of the Left Parties upon the local political scene. But this

autonomous expression of the dominated classes at the level of an
instrument which is part of the administration remains characterised
by the type of relations these classes have with it – which is structurally linked to the domination of a bloc of classes and factions, that
is to say, their expression is doubly subordinated: subordinated on
the one hand to the fundamental interests of the dominant bloc (in
Dunkirk, for example, the functioning of the complex unit of production could never in any way be called into question without grave
consequences); on the other hand, and this is crucial, it is subordinated to the pressure of the dominated classes, to struggles and political conflicts centred around urban problems. It is these practices
which determine the level and scope of the breaches introduced in
urban planning in relation to the structurally dominant logic.

The Social Function of Urban Planning

We can now understand the paradox which was our point of departure, for, if urban planning does not have much influence upon the
technical and national control of urban development, it has in
exchange very important effects upon those social relations which
are at the basis of this development. These effects occur basically
at two levels: at the ideological level in terms of the
rationalisation–legitimation of social interests, particularly through
planning documents; at the political level, as a privileged instrument of negotiation and mediation which all groups present attempt to appropriate in order to vest themselves with a social
and technical neutrality – this of course without planners themselves being able to change things in any way. Let us briefly re-
capitulate the results of our study at this point.

Planning documents appear in fact to be the formalisation of
projects of urban organisation, whose underlying social and
political logic we have been able to establish. The logic is different for each document and relates systematically to the evolution of political hegemony at the heart of the institutional
system on which each planning organism is based.

This hypothesis has proved itself to be so exact that certain
schemes, confronted with an uncertain political conjuncture,
have taken the shape of 'question-mark' schemes, and other
documents have evolved substantially according to the changing

political tendencies which control the planning apparatus – but more significant is the importance acquired by the ideological role of urban planning, because, for such an ideology to be efficient in the realisation of the social interests it formalises, the effect of 'legitimation–recognition', characteristic of all ideologies, must accommodate itself to the specific means of expression, which *is* urban planning.

Planning schemes vest particular projects with a double quality: on the one hand, they must become 'reasonable' rational technical solutions to given problems; on the other hand, they must (apparently) organise the convergence of different social interests and urban functions inside a coherent whole. Planning's technical usefulness will thus also acquire a social neutrality, composed of the general interests of the community. This is why urban planning is a privileged instrument for the ideological formalisation of interests of classes, fractions and groups, i.e. by developing the capacities for social integration to the maximum, which is the primary function of dominant ideology.

Moreover, as we have seen, the political role of urban planning is its ability to act as instrument of negotiation and mediation for, on the one hand, the dominant classes and their differing demands for the realisation of their common interests, and on the other the pressures and protests of the dominated classes. We have seen that this role of intermediary organism originates from the possibility of harmonising, within a relatively coherent framework, the central administration's various corrective and regulative interventions in situations where the dominant logic pushes contradictions so far that the process of the reproduction of labour and social relations becomes disordered.

However, for such a mediation to take place without altering the dominant structural logic, the dice must be loaded in some way, i.e. the very organisation of the process of negotiation must be such that once the various interests have been expressed they remain within the law. This effect is achieved through a number of mechanisms which vary from direct political control to administrative hierarchy and criteria for budgetary allocation.

It is this aptitude on the part of planning to be the context for conditioned and institutionalised social negotiation which explains the determination of various political tendencies to seize planning organisms which become not only political instruments but political stakes in themselves. This reveals the so often decried inability of urban and spatial planning to control growth and manage contradictions and collective consumption.

What becomes of planners under these conditions? Should they be strictly determined according to their assigned social function? No more and no less than any other social actor, i.e. they can attempt to bend the logic thus revealed through their attachments to other orientations or their relationship to other social practices, but these voluntary interventions (some would say 'voluntaristic') must take into account the limits within which they operate; and it is these limits their social origins, their political scope, their urban effects, which we have attempted to establish, beginning from the analysis of a concrete situation, which while being unique can also serve as an example.

Frustrated technician, unwitting ideologue and diplomat, the urban planner can also become the revealer of contradictions, and by this an agent of social innovation; but this is another story. If one wishes, one can form a scientific perspective and embark upon further research.

Appendix 1: Some Basic Data About the Dunkirk Region and about the Research

Evolution of Total Population (1936–68) and Projections (1975–85), Dunkirk Metropolitan Area

1936	1954	1962	1968	1975	1985
115,091	113,086	142,264	162,043	215,500	319,000

Annual Growth Rate (Estimate for 1985)

1936–54	1956–62	1962–68	1968–85
—0.1 per cent	+2.97 per cent	+2.04 per cent	+4.0 per cent

Social Composition of Active Population, 1968 (Percentage of Total Active Population)

Farmers	1.7
Agricultural workers	0.6
Commercial and industrial owners	10.1
Small shopkeepers	6.3

Hand craftsmen	3.0
Professionals and managers	4.2
Technicians and middle-rank professionals	9.2
Clerks	14.8
Workers (mostly industrial)	51.6
Skilled	20.5
Unskilled	24.0
Domestic service	5.9
Others	1.9

Major Corporations Located in Dunkirk

USINOR: first steel firm in France. The Dunkirk factory is producing 8 million tons of steel every year and will reach 16 million tons in 1980, 25 per cent of the whole steel production of France.
Creusot–Loira: metallurgy.
Chautiers Navals France Gironde: shipbuilding.
Vallourac: metallurgy.
B.P.: oil refinery.
Lesieur: peanut oil.
In addition, there are several electric plants and some subsidiary installations required by the steel industries.
In process of location: a major new oil refinery plus a huge plant of building materials plus a number of middle-size metallurgy industries.
In process of construction: a huge new super-harbour, with capacity for 500,000-ton tankers.

Evolution of Employment in the Five Big Firms in Dunkirk (Employees)

	1963	*1968*	*1970*	*1976*
Usinor	1250	4200	6600	12700
Creusot–Loire	1900	2250	2700	4800
Shipbuilding	2450	2250	2700	4550
B.P.	1300	1150	1050	1000
Lesieur	1000	900	900	900

Housing Situation, 1970

7000 people live in very bad slums

25 per cent of the population live in overcrowded housing

Indicators of housing (Dunkirk is a very new city; it was entirely destroyed during the war and rebuilt in 1945–50):

48 per cent of the total housing stock does not have hot water.

49 per cent of the total housing stock does not have W.C. inside the house.

70 per cent of the housing stock does not have central-heating system.

90 per cent of the housing stock does not have telephone.

Only 37 per cent of heads of households own their home (average in France 48 per cent).

To face new urban growth, 4000 new housing units a year are needed between 1970 and 1980. The average construction between 1960–70 was 1500 units each year. The actual figure in the 1970–5 programme was 3000 per year.

Local Politics

The Metropolitan Government is composed of eighteen communes.

The central city, Dunkirk (37,000 in 1968) is ruled by the UDR (Gaullists). The old peripheral communities are ruled by the socialist 'notables'. The new expanding working-class community is controlled, since 1971, by a coalition of Left-Socialists and Communists led by the Union Leader of steel-workers.

The old working-class communities (shoremen, railway workers) are led by local workers' leaders, mostly Communists (but their power is essentially charismatic: when they go out of the C.P. they keep control).

The Metropolitan Government was first under the control of socialist 'notables'. The chairman of the Metropolitan Government is the local 'boss' of the whole region, an old Right-wing Socialist. After 1971 he kept the chairmanship of the Metropolitan Government, but only with the support of Left Socialists and Communists. As a result, the key Urban Planning Committee is headed by the steel-workers' union leader and the Employment Committtee by the shoremen union's leader (a charismatic Communist worker).

Social Conflicts

Dunkirk is one of the areas in France with the highest level of working-class conflict: 55 per cent of workers in unions, with 20–25 per cent as the national average: the longest strike in 1968 was in USINOR (40 days); since 1968 there has been a continuous series of strikes, very often with violent clashes with the police and with the company's clerks for several days. When de Gaulle (1966) and the Prime Minister (1972) visited the city there was a general strike against the government.

The C.G.T. (the largest French union, Communist led) is very strong, but surprisingly the C.P. is not so strong. The C.F.D.T. (the second union) has become quite important, and so are the new trends (to the left) in the Socialist Party.

There were strong Maoists groups representing the young workers in 1968–72, but they were destroyed by heavy repression, both from the management and from the police.

The Research

Accomplished from January 1971 to July 1973 by a team of *three* full-time researchers (including myself) under my direction as a part of the Urban Research Programme of the Ecolé des Hautes Etudes. In addition, we were helped by several field-work researchers on a temporary base. One person lived in Dunkirk for six months. The whole team spent one week each month there for eighteen months. We gathered all the information available and we observed the functioning of local institutions, planning agencies, factories, the Port Authority, workers' unions, neighbourhood committees, and so on. The basic material of our research consisted of in-depth interviews with key informants (120 recorded interviews with a length of one to three hours). All important people in all fields were interviewed and their statements were cross-checked.

We had complete access to all information, since we were simultaneously introduced by the government, by the university, by the unions and by all tendencies of the Left political parties.

The research was funded by the government as a part of a programme to prepare the construction of urban simulation games. We selected Dunkirk because it was the major industrial–urban project going on in France and because we could directly observe a process of social and institutional change taking place at a particular moment in time.

Appendix 2: Glossary of Abbreviations

AGUR   Agence d'urbanisme
APEX   Association pour l'expansion industrielle
C.C.I.D.   Chambre de commerce et d'industrie de Dunkerque
C.D.E.E.S.   Comité dunkerquois d'études économiques et sociales
C.F.D.T.   Confédération française democratique du travail
DATAR   Délégation à l'aménagement du territoire et à l'action régionale (Prime Minister branch)
D.D.E.   Direction départementale de l'equipement (Ministry of Equipment)
G.C.P.U.   Groupe central de planification urbaine (Ministry of Equipment)
G.E.P.   Groupe d'etude et de programmation (Ministry of Equipment)
H.L.M.   Habitation a loyer modéré
M.E.L.   Ministère de l'équipement et du logement
OREAM   Organisation d'études d'aménagement de l'aire métropolitain (branch of central government)
ORETUR   Organisation d'études urbaines
P.A.D.   Port autonome de Dunkerque
P.O.S.   Plan d'occupation du sol
P.U.D.   Plan d'urbanisme de détail
S.D.A.U.   Schema directeur d'amenagement et d'urbanisme
SECADU   Syndicat mixte pour l'aménagement du littoral Calais-Dunkerque
U.D.R.   Union pour la défense de la republique (Gaullist party)
Z.U.P.   Zone à urbaniser en priorité

Chapter 5

Urban Renewal and Social Conflict

Introduction

'Urban problems' are increasingly becoming a political issue as the socialisation of the means of production is accompanied by the increasing socialisation of the means of consumption, or, if one prefers, from the moment collective facilities begin to play a strategic role in the structure and rhythms of everyday life.

It is to be expected that we should be witnessing growing administrative intervention in this field, whether to adjust the dysfunctioning of the urban structure (or, through it, of the social structure), or to carry out a policy whose evolution is capable of being oriented in favour of the long-term interests of the over-all social system of which administrative bodies are the institutional expression. Urban planning thus becomes the nerve centre of urban development, less as its motor than as a reflection of profound trends.

On the one hand, in as much as 'the city' is not a framework but a social practice in constant flux, the more it becomes an issue, the more it is a source of contradictions and the more its social manipulation is linked to the *ensemble* of social and political conflicts. A whole series of relationships thus grows up between the conflictual field, specifically linked to urban contradictions, and the conjuncture of social movements. By social movements we mean a certain type of organisation of social practices, the logic of whose development contradicts the institutionally dominant social logic. Consequently, research is faced with a series of problems. On the other hand, we must establish the social significance of urban planning interventions above and beyond the coherence of documents and urban plans, which are mostly ideological expressions. Furthermore, we must conceive of opposition to decisions relating to urban planning as something more than 'consumer-reaction' and, consequently, we must link it to the whole range of social contradictions and look into the conditions for the emergence and the determination of the objectives of social movements in the urban field. Finally, on a basis of the elements emerging from analysis on these two levels, we must study their specific articulation, i.e. the reciprocal interactions between urban planning interventions and the social dynamic in its different orientations: participationist, focused on demands, or contestatory.

We shall try to press forward with the concrete treatment of this set of problems through an examination of the process of urban renewal in Paris and through an analysis (largely exploratory for the moment) of the protest movements relating to it.[1]

The Social Content of Urban Renewal in Paris

The urban renewal programme is one of the most spectacular urban programmes to have been undertaken in Paris; it is certainly the one which has provoked the biggest public outcry.[2]

The renewal programme, in the strict sense of the term, has two essential characteristics:

(1) It concerns an already structured social space, of which it changes the form, the social content and/or function.

(2) It is based on public initiative, whatever the legal or financial form of the renewal agency, where private enterprise may take over the work, as in the case of *Opération Italie* (the urban renewal project of the Avenue d'Italie district in south Paris), though remaining within the over-all plan traced by city planning institutions. If other operations, limited in scope, carried out by private promoters, are sometimes related to the renewal programme, they are not as significant since – apart from the fact that they are not on the same scale – quantitatively they are not the expression of an over-all urbanistic logic as is the case with the renewal programme, which allows us to grasp the orientation of urban planning in relation to the area of the city of Paris.

This renewal programme, of which the first appreciable post-war achievements were set in motion in 1955–6, rapidly gathered speed up to the launching, in 1966, of a large Avenue d'Italie operation, which should take several years to complete; preparations are currently afoot to hand almost the entire operation over to the private sector. The proportions of the operation have become fairly modest since, of the 1500 hectares (3700 acres) which the City Council's Master Plan judged as requiring renewal, only 381.6 hectares (approx. 940 acres) have been involved in the operations undertaken between 1955 and 1 January 1970. All the same, this has produced considerable effects on the entire urban structure of Paris, given the strategic role of the renewed areas.[3]

To be objective, analysis of an urban programme such as the 'Reconquest of Paris' cannot be founded on speeches or on planners' projects, but should consider, rather, the transformations which it provokes in the areas affected by it. Based on the social content thus established, the study of the institutional processes whereby the programme is carried out becomes intelligible, for, beyond the descriptions of the actors' activities, we perceive the social determination of the interests being catered to by the various agencies.[4]

We should at once get rid of the notion of the renewal programme as a housing programme: the number of dwellings to be demolished is 29,059, to be replaced by 36,495, while, within the framework of private construction between 1954 and 1964, in Paris, 6000 demolished dwellings gave place to 52,500; at the same time, a further 41,000 were constructed without any prior demolition.

It seems, moreover, that despite urbanists' intentions, the essential aim of the present phase of the renewal programme is not, as was the case with some small operations early in the programme, the elimination of Paris slums. Figure 1 thus shows the very partial overlap between current renewal operations and the blocs classified in the category of highest degree of insalubrity. In order to try to determine the specificity of the areas renovated, we have made a statistical analysis of all the renewal operations completed or underway (on 1 January 1970) for which data were available (*i.e.* twenty-three out of a total of thirty operations). On the basis of this analysis,[5] it was established that:

(1) Even concerning those areas with a higher than average proportion of rundown and overcrowded dwellings, the most marked specification is supplied by the social categories occupying them rather than by their physical state (areas with a high proportion of Algerians and semi-skilled and unskilled workers and a very low proportion of occupants from the professional and executive strata).

(2) There is a direct rank correlation between the size of the operation and these social stratification variables along with an inverse correlation between the size of the operation undertaken and the variables concerning the level of housing deterioration; that is to say, the

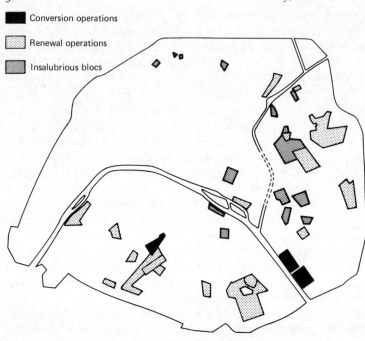

Conversion operations

Renewal operations

Insalubrious blocs

FIGURE I   *Renewal and unsalubrious blocs*

more insalubrious the district, the smaller the operation, while the more the district is inhabited by lower social strata the greater the dimensions of the renewal programme.

Finally, the central *arrondissements* of Paris, which are among the most dilapidated, are barely affected by the programme.

Furthermore, as against the explicitly stated goals of the Master Plan, the renewal programme is not going to make any significant contribution to an improvement in the capital's public facilities, that is, if one is to believe certain partial results which we have obtained, despite the difficulties in evaluating programmes whose essential portions have not yet been completed.

Concerning two essential facilities (schools and open spaces), it will be seen, from an analysis of programmes supplied by the renewal bodies themselves, and from our (deliberately underestimated) projections that:

(1) The renewal programme is not providing any new school

facilities, limiting itself to covering, at an average threshold, the needs of the new population. In certain cases (the 13th and 19th *arrondissements*) it is even taking advantage of already existing facilities (slightly less overcrowded than elsewhere), thus saturating them to the same level as in the rest of Paris.

(2) 56 per cent of the renewed surface will be below the Paris average in open space (0.8 m² per inhabitant) and 21 per cent will be above the current average but without reaching the minimum facility threshold laid down by the Master Plan itself.

What, then, is the social logic behind this programme?

To discover this we have studied, on the one hand, the social and functional characteristics of the area before its renewal from the point of view of their specificity in relation to Paris as a whole; on the other hand, instead of the post-renewal area (which only exists very partially so far) we have studied the social, functional and symbolic (the latter in outline only) content of current renewal programmes, where these prefigure the areas being constructed. First, the Paris area was divided into three operational categories defined by the variables chosen as indicators of social status, physical environment, economic function or political–institutional orientation. Next, the renewal operations now under way were attributed to these categories, using the number of hectares under renewal as the statistical unit. To study the content of the renewal programmes we have also selected a certain number of variables (for example, the proportion of H.L.M. housing to the total number of dwellings constructed within the operation) and distributed the totality of operations in surface units among the different categories of each variable.

Rather than give a detailed commentary on the tables corresponding to each analysis, we present a single, condensed table, whose advantage lies in its power of synthesis and whose inconvenience lies in its complexity (*cf.* Table 2). It is derived from systematic cross-tabulation of the principal results of the two series of observations we have just set out: the distribution of renewal operations among the values of the variables characterising the Paris area[6] and the distribution of these operations among the values of the variables characterising the content of the renewal programmes under way. This, then, is an indirect manner of comparing the pre-renewal area with what one might be justified in taking to be the content of the renewed space.

By examining Table 2 we know how many renovated

hectares correspond to each category of the entire programme defined in relation to the different variables dealt with. Since we dispose of the marginals for each cross-tabulation we can deduce the values for all the cells, and by standardising them relative to the total area renewed we obtain the proportion of surface renewed possessing both characteristics at the same time. By comparing the various probabilities among them, we can deduce approximately the differential influence of each element relative to the renewal scheme, and thus approach the discovery of its meaning. The marginal probabilities resume, comparatively, the differentiation introduced by each variable into the renewal scheme. We can thus make a very summary comparison of the respective influence of each factor.[7]

For example, let i be the characteristic 'high proportion of Algerians in the area before renewal' (with its complementary $\bar{\imath}$) and j the characteristic 'high proportion of municipal housing in the programme' (with its complementary $\bar{\jmath}$). By dichotomising and cross-tabulating, we obtain the following schema in which Pij is the probability of renewal of a certain urban sector of type i affected by an operation whose characteristic is j.

Proportion of Algerians (i)

		High	Low	
		High	Low	
Proportion of H.L.M. housing (j)	High	a P_{ij}	b $P_{\bar{\imath}j}$	$p.j$
	Low	c $P_{i\bar{\jmath}}$	d $P_{\bar{\imath}\bar{\jmath}}$	$p.\bar{\jmath}$
		$p_{i}.$	$p_{\bar{\imath}}.$	

$$N = a + b + c + d$$
$$p = 1$$

$$P_{ij} = P_i \times P_j = \frac{(a + c)\,(a + b)}{N}$$

It is clear that the 'probabilities' merely extrapolate from current trends and that they are not 'ineluctable'. They serve, however, to reveal the relative importance of the renewal programme in relation to the different elements studied. We shall not comment on the table in detail, but will limit ourselves to spelling out the social significance which emerges.

What is immediately striking is the systematic tendency of renewal logic to act as an extension of 'spontaneous' trends (*i.e.* determined along the general lines of social evolution) in the urban system of the Paris region; this is so at all levels.

It develops and accentuates residential segregation, extending the occupation of the city of Paris by the higher social strata, forcing the lower classes into the underequipped suburbs. This model of urban segregation, linked to the cultural, historical and functional role of Paris, is tending increasingly to reduce to secondary importance the historical East/West opposition.

Still more important is the fact that the renewal programme not only facilitates the reproduction of the specialisation of productive space but even accentuates this process. *Even though the constant increase in office space in Paris – now becoming a gigantic tertiary centre – is above all, the expression of the division of labour and of the constitution of the great monopoly capitalist organisations,* this tendency is none the less considerably re-enforced by the activities of the agencies responsible for the renewal programme.

The current consecration and development of Parisian 'centrality' – which is now being extended to the whole of the city and is affecting the region and the whole of the country, Europe not being beyond the reach of its ambitions – has made it necessary to regulate the channels of functional exchange, urban flux and creation of commercial centres. The transport programme, established at *district* level,[8] takes care of the first aspect; the launching of the new *commercial centres* (which, it is hoped, will at the same time grow into *cultural symbolic senders*, disseminating consumption values) devolves upon the renewal programme. This whole development is in line with current social trends, *i.e.* following the spatial logic of the most dynamic sectors of international monopoly capitalism.

Finally, the few elements available to us concerning urban symbolism also point in the direction of the reproduction of social tendencies at the level of urban forms with the qualification, however, that these are the most advanced tendencies within the dominant logic. In this way, for example, towers, the expression of those forms most charged with technocratic values (modernity, efficiency, rationality) will take precedence over conservative forms (stone-faced buildings, for example).

TABLE 2 *The change of Parisian space by operations of urban renewal: proportion of the surface renewed according to the pre-renewal characteristics of the space and according to those of the renewal operations (see notes on p. 102)*

Pre-renewal characteristics of renewed space: population

Functional characteristics of space allocation		Old people H	M	L	Young people H	M	L	Algerians H	M	L
H.L.M. housing	H	0	0.004	0.160	0.043	0.077	0.045	0.113	0	0.051
	M	0	0.005	0.169	0.046	0.082	0.047	0.120	0	0.054
	L	0	0.019	0.640	0.173	0.310	0.180	0.455	0	0.204
Offices	H	0	0.018	0.606	0.164	0.293	0.170	0.431	0	0.193
	L	0	0.011	0.363	0.098	0.176	0.102	0.255	0	0.116
Shops	H	0	0.012	0.390	0.105	0.189	0.110	0.278	0	0.124
	M	0	0.009	0.303	0.082	0.147	0.085	0.215	0	0.097
	L	0	0.008	0.275	0.074	0.113	0.077	0.195	0	0.088
Tower blocks	H	0	0.016	0.572	0.155	0.277	0.161	0.407	0	0.182
	L	0	0.012	0.397	0.107	0.192	0.111	0.282	0	0.187
Open space	H	0	0.006	0.218	0.059	0.105	0.061	0.155	0	0.069
	M	0	0.006	0.203	0.055	0.098	0.057	0.144	0	0.065
	L	0	0.016	0.548	0.148	0.265	0.152	0.389	0	0.175
Schools	H	0	0.003	0.106	0.028	0.051	0.030	0.075	0	0.034
	M	0	0.008	0.261	0.071	0.126	0.073	0.186	0	0.082
	L	0	0.018	0.601	0.163	0.291	0.169	0.427	0	0.192
Over-all marginal probabilities		0	0.330	0.970	0.263	0.470	0.273	0.690	0	0.310

Pre-renewal characteristics of renewed space: urban structure

Functional characteristics of space allocation		Office density H	L	Office space increase H	M	L	Industrial density H	M	L	Area served by industry H	M	L	Size of shops H	M	L
H.L.M. housing	H	0.024	0.124	0.077	0.024	0.062	0.106	0.058	0	0.131	0.033	0	0	0	0.165
	M	0.026	0.131	0.082	0.026	0.066	0.112	0.062	0	0.140	0.035	0	0	0	0.175
	L	0.099	0.495	0.310	0.099	0.025	0.425	0.234	0	0.527	0.132	0	0	0	0.660
Offices	H	0.093	0.468	0.293	0.093	0.237	0.403	0.221	0	0.499	0.125	0	0	0	0.625
	L	0.056	0.281	0.176	0.056	0.145	0.241	0.133	0	0.299	0.075	0	0	0	0.375
Shops	H	0.060	0.302	0.189	0.060	0.153	0.259	0.143	0	0.322	0.081	0	0	0	0.403
	M	0.046	0.234	0.147	0.046	0.119	0.201	0.110	0	0.250	0.063	0	0	0	0.313
	L	0.042	0.213	0.113	0.042	0.105	0.183	0.100	0	0.227	0.057	0	0	0	0.284
Tower blocks	H	0.088	0.442	0.277	0.088	0.224	0.380	0.244	0	0.471	0.118	0	0	0	0 500
	L	0.061	0.307	0.192	0.061	0.155	0.264	0.145	0	0.327	0.082	0	0	0	0.410
Open space	H	0.033	0.168	0.105	0.033	0.085	0.145	0.079	0	0.180	0.045	0	0	0	0.225
	M	0.031	0.157	0.098	0.031	0.079	0.135	0.074	0	0.167	0.042	0	0	0	0.210
	L	0.084	0.423	0.265	0.084	0.214	0.364	0.200	0	0.451	0.113	0	0	0	0.565
Schools	H	0.016	0.082	0.051	0.016	0.041	0.070	0.039	0	0.087	0.022	0	0	0	0.110
	M	0.040	0.202	0.126	0.040	0.102	0.174	0.096	0	0.216	0.054	0	0	0	0.270
	L	0.093	0.465	0.291	0.093	0.235	0.340	0.220	0	0.495	0.124	0	0	0	0.620
Over-all marginal probabilities		0.150	0.750	0.047	0.150	0.380	0.645	0.355	0	0.799	0.201	0	0	0	1

Foreigners			Semi-skilled and unskilled workers			Professionals and executives			Artisans and shopkeepers		
H	M	L	H	M	L	H	M	L	H	M	L
0.006	0.010	0.148	0.116	0.047	0.001	0	0.007	0.157	0.051	0.067	0.045
0.007	0.011	0.157	0.183	0.070	0.001	0	0.008	0.167	0.055	0.071	0.048
0.026	0.039	0.594	0.465	0.187	0.006	0	0.029	0.630	0.207	0.268	0.181
0.025	0.037	0.562	0.441	0.177	0.006	0	0.028	0.596	0.196	0.254	0.171
0.015	0.022	0.337	0.264	0.106	0.003	0	0.016	0.368	0.118	0.118	0.103
0.016	0.024	0.362	0.284	0.114	0.004	0	0.018	0.384	0.126	0.164	0.110
0.012	0.018	0.281	0.220	0.089	0.003	0	0.013	0.298	0.098	0.127	0.085
0.011	0.017	0.255	0.200	0.080	0.002	0	0.012	0.270	0.089	0.115	0.050
0.023	0.035	0.531	0.416	0.167	0.005	0	0.026	0.563	0.185	0.240	0.162
0.016	0.024	0.369	0.289	0.116	0.004	0	0.018	0.391	0.129	0.166	0.112
0.009	0.013	0.202	0.158	0.063	0.002	0	0.010	0.214	0.069	0.091	0.061
0.008	0.012	0.189	0.148	0.059	0.002	0	0.009	0.200	0.066	0.085	0.057
0.022	0.033	0.518	0.398	0.160	0.005	0	0.025	0.529	0.177	0.229	0.155
0.004	0.006	0.099	0.077	0.031	0.001	0	0.004	0.104	0.034	0.044	0.030
0.010	0.016	0.243	0.191	0.076	0.002	0	0.012	0.257	0.085	0.109	0.074
0.024	0.037	0.558	0.437	0.176	0.006	0	0.027	0.592	0.195	0.252	0.170
0.040	0.060	0.900	0.706	0.284	0.010	0	0.045	0.955	0.315	0.407	0.275

Type* of shops			Concentration of shops			Commercial capacity†			Metro facilities‡			Price per m² old dwellings			Price per m² recent dwellings		
H	M	L	H	M	L	H	M	L	H	M	L	H	M	L	H	M	L
0	0.011	0.153	0	0	0.165	0	0	0.165	0.033	0.112	0.021	0	0.024	0.140	0	0.094	0.070
0	0.012	0.162	0	0	0.022	0	0	0.175	0.035	0.119	0.022	0	0.026	0.148	0	0.099	0.075
0	0.046	0.613	0	0	0.660	0	0	0.660	0.132	0.448	0.085	0	0.099	0.561	0	0.376	0.283
0	0.043	0.584	0	0	0.625	0	0	0.625	0.118	0.425	0.081	0	0.093	0.531	0	0.356	0.268
0	0.026	0.348	0	0	0.375	0	0	0.375	0.071	0.255	0.048	0	0.057	0.318	0	0.213	0.166
0	0.028	0.374	0	0	0.403	0	0	0.403	0.080	0.274	0.052	0	0.060	0.342	0	0.219	0.173
0	0.021	0.291	0	0	0.313	0	0	0.313	0.062	0.212	0.040	0	0.046	0.266	0	0.178	0.134
0	0.019	0.264	0	0	0.284	0	0	0.284	0.056	0.193	0.036	0	0.042	0.241	0	0.161	0.122
0	0.041	0.548	0	0	0.590	0	0	0.590	0.118	0.401	0.076	0	0.088	0.501	0	0.336	0.253
0	0.028	0.381	0	0	0.410	0	0	0.410	0.082	0.278	0.053	0	0.061	0.348	0	0.233	0.176
0	0.015	0.209	0	0	0.225	0	0	0.225	0.045	0.153	0.029	0	0.033	0.191	0	0.128	0.096
0	0.014	0.195	0	0	0.210	0	0	0.210	0.042	0.142	0.027	0	0.031	0.178	0	0.119	0.090
0	0.039	0.526	0	0	0.565	0	0	0.565	0.113	0.348	0.073	0	0.084	0.480	0	0.322	0.242
0	0.007	0.102	0	0	0.110	0	0	0.110	0.022	0.074	0.014	0	0.016	0.093	0	0.062	0.047
0	0.018	0.254	0	0	0.270	0	0	0.270	0.054	0.183	0.035	0	0.040	0.229	0	0.153	0.116
0	0.043	0.575	0	0	0.620	0	0	0.620	0.124	0.421	0.080	0	0.093	0.527	0	0.353	0.266
0	0.070	0.093	0	0	1	0	0	1	0.200	0.680	0.120	0	0.150	0.850	0	0.570	0.430

(continued overleaf)

TABLE 2 *(continued)*

Pre-renewal characteristics of renewed space

Functional characteristics of space allocation		Housing								
		Overcrowding			Dwellings without water			Left vote in municipal elections		
		H	M	L	H	M	L	H	M	L
H.L.M. housing	H	0.136	0.003	0.024	0.037	0.026	0.100	0.118	0.046	0
	M	0.145	0.003	0.025	0.040	0.028	0.106	0.126	0.049	0
	L	0.547	0.013	0.097	0.151	0.105	0.400	0.475	0.184	0
Offices	H	0.518	0.012	0.092	0.143	0.100	0.379	0.450	0.175	0
	L	0.311	0.007	0.055	0.086	0.060	0.238	0.210	0.185	0
Shops	H	0.344	0.008	0.059	0.092	0.064	0.244	0.290	0.112	0
	M	0.259	0.006	0.046	0.072	0.053	0.189	0.225	0.087	0
	L	0.235	0.005	0.042	0.065	0.045	0.172	0.204	0.079	0
Tower blocks	H	0.489	0.011	0.087	0.135	0.094	0.356	0.424	0.165	0
	L	0.340	0.008	0.060	0.093	0.065	0.248	0.295	0.114	0
Open space	H	0.186	0.004	0.037	0.051	0.036	0.136	0.162	0.063	0
	M	0.154	0.004	0.031	0.048	0.029	0.127	0.151	0.058	0
	L	0.468	0.011	0.083	0.119	0.090	0.342	0.406	0.158	0
Schools	H	0.091	0.002	0.016	0.025	0.017	0.066	0.079	0.030	0
	M	0.224	0.005	0.039	0.062	0.043	0.163	0.194	0.083	0
	L	0.514	0.020	0.091	0.142	0.099	0.376	0.446	0.173	0
Over-all probabilities		0.830	0.020	0.148	0.230	0.160	0.607	0.720	0.280	0

* Proportion of daily to occasional consumption shops.
† This indicator is based on the number of shop employees per thousand inhabitants.
‡ Metro facility: an index based on network density and proximity to stations.
¶ U.D.R. (Union des Démocrates pour la Vᵉ République, the Gaullist party); 'safety' is based on proportion of votes cast for the party in the two parts of elections.
§ 'Stronghold' indicates that party obtains a majority of votes without dependence on electoral alliances.

Notes
Unit of counting: hectares under renewal.
Counting procedure: total hectares equal to 1; proportions (on the basis of the unit) calculated out of the total of hectares.
Symbols: H – high proportion of the characteristic indicated
M – average proportion of the characteristic indicated
L – low proportion of the characteristic indicated
Probabilities of occurrence: cells divided by N; *standardisation:* $N = 1$. *Construction of variables:* (a) pre-renewal space variables: see note 5; (b) functional characteristics of urban-renewal operations: each operation has been ranked in comparison with the content of the renewal programme as a whole.
Acknowledgement: This table was elaborated by Francis Godard.

Institutional system									
Communist strength			*Safe for U.D.R.*¶			*Stronghold of U.D.R.*§			*Over-all marginal probabilities*
H	M	L	H	M	L	H	M	L	
0.118	0.028	0.019	0.006	0.035	0.124	0.010	0.037	0.090	0.165
0.126	0.030	0.019	0.007	0.037	0.131	0.011	0.060	0.100	0.175
0.475	0.112	0.072	0.026	0.138	0.495	0.041	0.231	0.386	0.660
0.450	0.106	0.068	0.025	0.131	0.468	0.040	0.218	0.366	0.627
0.276	0.063	0.041	0.015	0.078	0.281	0.040	0.131	0.219	0.375
0.290	0.068	0.044	0.016	0.084	0.302	0.025	0.141	0.236	0.403
0.225	0.053	0.034	0.012	0.065	0.234	0.019	0.085	0.183	0.313
0.204	0.048	0.031	0.011	0.059	0.213	0.017	0.099	0.166	0.284
0.424	0.100	0.064	0.023	0.123	0.442	0.038	0.206	0.345	0.590
0.295	0.069	0.045	0.016	0.086	0.307	0.025	0.143	0.240	0.410
0.162	0.038	0.020	0.009	0.047	0.168	0.014	0.068	0.131	0.225
0.151	0.035	0.023	0.008	0.044	0.157	0.013	0.073	0.123	0.210
0.406	0.096	0.062	0.022	0.118	0.423	0.035	0.907	0.331	0.569
0.079	0.018	0.012	0.004	0.023	0.082	0.006	0.038	0.064	0.110
0.194	0.045	0.020	0.010	0.056	0.202	0.017	0.094	0.158	0.270
0.446	0.105	0.068	0.024	0.130	0.465	0.039	0.217	0.363	0.620
0.720	0.170	0.110	0.040	0.210	0.750	0.030	0.350	0.586	

Sources: The *population* and *housing* data were taken from the 1962 census. The figures concerning the *arrondissements* and *îlots* (census tracts or blocs) were obtained from INSEE (Institut National de la Statistique et des Études Économiques).

Data for the *spatial variables* were found in: J. Beaujeu and J. Bastié, *Atlas de la Région Parisienne* (Paris: Berger-Levrault, 1967); in the *Schéma directeur de la ville de Paris* and in documents available at APUR (Atelier Parisien d'Urbanisme).

The years of reference are the following for the different indicators for 'urban structure':

1962   'office density', 'industrial density'.

1962–8 'office space increase', 'outflow of industry'.

1966   The four indicators concerning commercial equipment, the 'metro facility' indicator and the square metre price of dwellings.

The electoral data for the 'institutional system' indicators concern the municipal and parliamentary elections of 1966 and 1967.

The 'Reconquest of Paris' constitutes, then, without any doubt, an intervention by the state apparatus in space, aimed at the extended reproduction of the Paris region's urban system, in terms of its 'centrality', of the managerial units of the productive machine and of urban stratification.

Why Urban Renewal in Paris? The Political Background of Urban Planning

The problem now facing us is why state intervention should be necessary in order to give further impetus to the development of social trends whose strength is already observable. If it is true that the over-concentration of central functions necessitates some regulatory intervention, the renewal programme appears, rather, to act as an accelerator of the process. Consequently, rather than a response to a crisis in the urban system, it appears to be an initiative emanating primarily from the state apparatus and should hence be examined from the point of view of the internal logic of politics.

Since administrative (or, more generally, state) intervention can be analysed in terms of its impact on the economy, on the politico–institutional structure (*i.e.* itself), on ideology, or, more directly, on social relations, the totality of its significance can be laid bare within the relationship between urban renewal and the various institutions mentioned. Our research necessarily becomes far more hesitant at this point, but we would like to suggest some hypotheses liable to spark off the debate.

Since the renewal programme is producing no new impact on the economy or on the functioning of the Paris region's urban structure, in which it limits itself, rather, to broadening existing trends, some people might conclude that this constitutes a simple case of the large organisations and real-estate firms heavily influencing the urban planning bodies. Such a direct assimilation of politico–administrative institutions to private economic interests, even if it has a certain historical foundation, seems to us to be a little too schematic, leaving the essential role of the state out of account. To progress further with our analysis, we must broaden the logic of this intervention beyond simple reproduction of Parisian space, *i.e.* we must consider the effects produced on the other institutions.

On the level of the *institutional system*, one certain effect of the renewal programme has been to modify the orientation of the electorate

through population change: the renewal programme has been striking, above all, those zones where the Left is well established and the
majority is either outnumbered or threatened. It is clear that electoral
behaviour is linked to the social characteristics of the resident population (workers, low income level, etc.) and that its modification is not
intentionally a prime consideration. None the less, the replacement of
workers by executives produces the anticipated effect on the city's
political representation, which is obviously highly significant socially.
It remains to be explained, however, just why electoral control of the
city of Paris is such an important issue.

We can further strengthen our understanding of the 'Reconquest of
Paris' by introducing in the analysis the role played by prestige operations on the level of the diffusion of ideological messages. The signify-
ing of France's new greatness and the confirmation of the choice of
Paris as place of residence of the headquarters of large, Euro-
pean-scale companies seem to combine to make Paris a show-case
both of a certain prosperity and of a strong capacity for state initiative
at the level of environmental improvement, consecrating Paris's position as business centre and cultural sender for the whole of Europe.

None the less, the ideological labelling of an area is never an end in
itself, in so far as ideological sending only exists through the effect it
produces on its audience. In other words, this effect of ideological
demonstration, as well as the interference with the composition of the
Paris electorate, seems to be aimed at acting on *social relations, i.e.* on
the linking up of the content of Paris with the dynamic of social
classes. We enter, here, into the world of the hypothetical, but all
analysis seems to converge on this point, one which is far harder to
grasp, concretely, than any of the findings established up to now. In
short, why do class relations depend on the occupation of a certain
area? Why is it significant that the majority (Gaullist) controls the
city of Paris rather than the suburbs or the provinces?

We will venture to advance two hypotheses.

(1) The first concerns the *political conjuncture* in France. Since 1958,
the ruling classes have attempted, under the protection of a great
leader, to create a stable hegemonic party, with roots in the population and the electorate. If this electoral base has been established,
through a variety of subtle combinations made possible by strategically suitable conjunctures, the party still very definitely lacks
roots in all strata of the population, especially at the local level. The

municipal councils are in the hands of the working classes and their representatives, or in those of the traditional bourgeoisie and petty bourgeoisie. It has become a matter of urgency to possess solid local ramifications now that the charismatic leader is dead, so that a majority party can be solidly constructed on some base other than arbitrage between the different currents in French political life. The electoral assault on the large provincial cities has to be made from the outside, as in the case of Toulouse, or by means of a pact with the system of local domination, as for instance in Lyon. Paris, however, which is not administratively autonomous *vis-à-vis* the government, offers a privileged terrain for long-term action, gradually transforming the city, then allowing a wide degree of local initiative in order, at the appropriate moment, to have a base of popular support for a great 'modern' conservative party.[9]

(2) We should also take into account the role played by Paris in the *history of political conflict* in France. One thinks immediately of the Commune, but, closer to us in time, the May 1968 movement was narrowly linked to its Paris environment; the initial support of the population, its partial change of heart later, played a very great part in the events. But, it may be asked, why should this struggle take place in the central part of the city rather than in factories, for example, or the working-class suburbs?

If we restrict the May movement to its most radical expression, the Leftist movement, it may be said that the importance of Paris stems from the particular conditions of its organisation, or, rather, its disorganisation. The slogan 'Power lies in the streets' was not only an ideological key-note, it was a rallying cry. In other words, the movement, in its fragmented state (then as now), saw the occupation of the streets, demonstrations and public assembly as the only organic forms it could adopt, in the absence of any 'hegemonic' party or 'political front'.

Consequently, a Paris occupied by the higher social strata, a showcase of comfort and modernity, is a Paris cut off from potential outbursts of protest, which will be doomed to oscillate between a scattering of struggles among a variety of trouble spots and direct confrontation with the forces of repression in the political isolation of a transformed capital.

Obviously, there is no question of a highly clairvoyant ruling class consciously planning all this, but it does seem as though the effects of the renewal programme are pointing in this direction; in consequence they are perceived as positive in other forms, sometimes veiled by the ideology of those in whose interest the programme is working. Even if the representatives of a social class are not always capable of recognising themselves, the class itself discovers its interests, in the sense that its logic unconsciously tends to sweep aside anything that is not useful to it.

On the other hand, the renewal programme is not that alone. It is, above all, an enlarged reproduction of the Paris region's urban system in the direction described, and in this respect it fulfills the social logic underlying the economic structure of the Paris region. What needs to be explained is why there is coincidence between economic and class interests directly expressed, spatially, in the logic of the state apparatus, to which we attribute a relative autonomy. We think this coincidence and mutual strengthening can be explained by the effects of the renewal programme on *social relations*, in other words by its redoubled effects on the economy, the politico–institutional structure and on ideology.

Finally, it is true that it is a long way from the modest proportions of the renewal programme to the scale of the implicit objectives we are attributing to it. But the programme is playing a pilot role, opening the breach in the working class areas and creating the conditions in which private enterprise can continue and multiply its activities in this direction. This is the way in which we should look at the increasingly marked tendency to hand over to private contractors and at the development of 'concerted-action' procedures.[10]

Figure 2 summarises – 'schematically', certainly – both the significance of the renewal process such as we have described it and the hypotheses advanced in order to discover the missing links in the chain.

What we have analysed up to now is the *tendential social logic* of an urban planning operation. But a society is not a reproduction of structurally dominant social tendencies. It is also a locus of change, collective mobilisation or the defence of group interests and, consequently, is a confrontation of goals. All the same, this mobilisation does not occur in a social vacuum: it threads itself into the web of a structurally determined set of problems. Having grasped the social significance of Parisian renewal, in the sense of a process taking place within a certain structural logic, we must analyse how it has been deflected by the activities of groups and social forces whose developmental logic differs from that which lies behind the renewal programme. We should also analyse how the content of this programme affects the organisation and development of social movements for whom this is at issue.

The Reverse Side of the Urban-renewal Programme: from Protest to Social Movement

The movements protesting the impact of the Paris renewal programme are both too hesitant and too diversified for us to be able to synthesise their meaning and produce a theoretical interpretation. Their detailed description being, on the other hand, too complex to be exposed within the framework of this article, we have decided to summarise the fundamental traits of the different conflicts which developed around a single sector of the renewal programme in order to demonstrate the emergence and transformation of these new types of social movement through the example of one case.

There is no question of generalising from this, but observations carried out on other Parisian sectors permit us to consider the mechanisms observed as characteristic of a *specific process*: the fight against the renewal programme and, in particular, the fight for the right to housing threatened by the programme.[11]

The sector we have chosen for our analysis, which we will call *Cité-du-Peuple*, presents certain specific characteristics (social and ecological). Table 3 summarises the most important characteristics of the whole sector and of the two areas of the sector in which the process studied took place.

The sector is an old lower-class area, with a high proportion of workers, a heavy concentration of ethnic communities and immigrant labourers. The site offers some considerable advantages for any eventual high-class housing scheme, and its proximity to the expanding business district creates the basic conditions for an 'urban-reconquest' operation aimed at changing the physical, social, functional and symbolic aspects of land occupation.

Two types of urban renewal have followed in succession: the first, starting slowly in 1958, was aimed at the demolition of a few insalubrious blocs, in a particularly run-down condition. The second movement, which began to pick up speed around 1965–6 and which is currently in full-swing, aimed above all at the kind of transformation typical of 'urban-reconquest' operations.

The accentuation of this orientation and, consequently, the

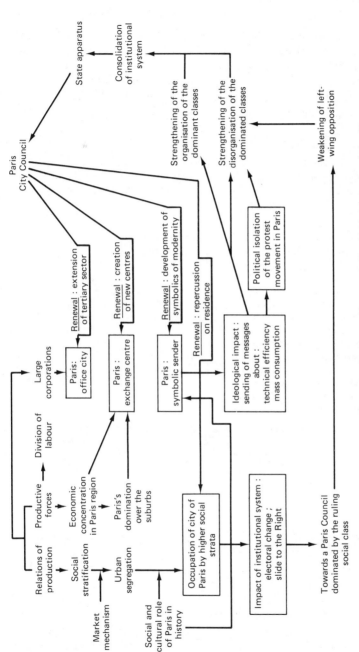

FIGURE 2 *The social logic of the Paris urban renewal programme*
(findings and hypotheses)

* Arrows bearing on arrows indicate interaction, *i.e.* an effect not on the variable but on the relationship; *direct* effects of the urban-renewal programme are indicated by the use of boxes.

speeding-up of the rate of construction, provoked a shift in the preoccupations and demands of the population concerned. The demand for decent housing at a reasonable rent and close to the place of work has taken second place in the face of the threat of expulsion, in face of the overriding fear of finding oneself without lodging, obliged to accept quarters in transit housing facilities.

TABLE 3   *Socio-economic characteristics and living conditions in the Cité-du-Peuple in relation to the Paris average and in the two quarters in relation to the 'Cité-du-Peuple' as a whole, in 1962 (indexes of differentiation)**

Percentage	Cité-du-Peuple	Square Gaieté	Presqu'île
Population more than 65-years-old	− 0.22	+ 0.13	0
Population less than 19-years-old	+ 0.09	− 0.11	− 0.09
Algerians	+ 0.90	− 0.77	+ 0.10
Foreigners	− 0.11	− 0.13	+ 0.61
Semi- and unskilled workers	+ 0.54	− 0.13	+ 0.14
Executives and professionals	− 0.50	− 0.06	− 0.30
Artisans and shopkeepers	− 0.24	+ 0.30	0
Active population	+ 0.01	+ 0.07	− 0.10
Persons living in overcrowded conditions	+ 0.36	+ 0.30	+ 0.76
Dwellings without water	0	+ 0.44	+ 0.58
Dwellings without W.C.	+ 0.08	− 0.10	+ 0.75
Active women	− 0.09	0	0

* The indexes of differentiation have been calculated as follows:

$$\frac{\text{Percentage value for each variable in urban area studied}}{\text{Corresponding percentage value in larger area used as unit of reference}} - 1$$

Consequently, 0 means no difference; + or − indicate the direction of the difference.

From spontaneous reactions to organised intervention, whether political or focused on specific demands, a certain mobilisation took place around the question of being able to remain in one's dwelling so long as no satisfactory offer, in terms of a combination of dimensions, comfort, price and location, had been received. What was at issue in all the different actions engaged in, in the *Cité-du-Peuple*, was a common factor, namely the contradiction between, on the one hand, the *housing conditions* of the population concerned and, on the other, the

Paris urban-renewal project (on the social, functional and symbolic levels) *adapted to the benefit of the real-estate promoters.* However, the first pole (concerning the 'population') covers a diversity of situations (tenant, lodger, owner, co-owner, shopkeeper, etc.) and can ultimately be broken down into terms of intense contradictions (for example, between owners and tenants).

If the objective *issues* coincide, the particularities of the social base concerned in each sector and the *type of intervention* originating the mobilisation process produce a variety of forms of struggle, depending on a large range of political situations and urban structures. It is this *ensemble* of specific processes that we are trying to explain, basing ourselves, in particular, on an analysis of the two areas of the *Cité-du-Peuple* in which the mobilisation was more marked than elsewhere and where a variety of orientations underwent trial by practice. The areas, which we have called *Square Gaieté* and *Presqu'île*, are quite distinct from one another, as appears from their characterisation in Table 3.

Defending the Worker's Everyday Life: Square Gaieté

Square Gaieté was, for several years, the meeting-place for all the protest actions of the area. These have centred, above all, around the demand for the construction of low-rent housing in the sector. Having been backed up by a nation-wide *tenants' association*, the protest actions were powerfully aided by the ever-growing threat which the renewal programme posed to the inhabitants of the area.

For over five years, up till 1966–7, weekly mobilisations took place, with door-to-door campaigns, petitions, delegations and numerous meetings backed by the parties and the unions, even going to the lengths of street demonstrations with the participation of thousands of inhabitants.

At the present time, the 2000-odd H.L.M. dwellings have been constructed and occupied in the place provided for. At first sight, then, this broad protest action, demanding the construction of low-rent housing which began with an essentially working-class mobilisation confronting the public authorities (the Prefect, the Paris City Council, the O.H.L.M. responsible for public facilities and housing) has been successful and that *on the occasion* of the urban-renewal process. What concerns us here is to establish the meaning of this kind of action as a social process and, consequently, to measure its impact in terms of the actors themselves and of the entire social dynamic thus engaged.

The essential point is the following: if H.L.M. housing was in fact constructed (one-half the number demanded during the protest campaign) *the immense majority of the area's threatened population, the broad base of the mobilisation, was not rehoused in these dwellings*. The reason for this is quite simple: it stems from the administrative mechanism for the attribution of H.L.M. housing, which must adhere to a waiting-list which covers the entire department. Consequently, the housing obtained by the struggle of the *Cité-du-Peuple's* residents was given to badly housed families from any part of Paris who had been waiting for years. There is, then, an incompatibility between the basis for mobilisation and the possible response to the claims, since the central administration cannot bypass the attributive mechanism. Hence, if it is clear that we can envisage local actions taking position on broad policy issues (in the same way that the workers in one factory can strike in order to defeat a national stabilisation plan) we should remember that the mobilisation's *raison d'être* was to supply dwellings for a group of people fighting an expulsion procedure. It was this situation which underlay the capacity for mobilisation.

There was, however, a demand which would have been capable of re-establishing the link between the situation underlying the problem and the goal to be attained: the request for a multiple-stage operation within the framework of each operation under the renewal programme: in other words, construction prior to demolition, on the same sites, in order to rehouse the expelled families at reasonable rents. This kind of demand, however, runs completely counter to the very foundations of the whole renewal undertaking, which is aimed, above all, at solidly transforming the area and introducing a strong consumption dynamic (which would require greater purchasing power) along with a symbolic labelling (linked to the social status of the residents). Here, then, is an issue in which residents threatened with expulsion are directly confronted with the powerful machine of the Paris urban-renewal programme.

This demand certainly figured prominently in the campaign we have just described. But, its nature being very different from the simple demand for the construction of H.L.M. housing (which barely touched the renewal programme itself), it would have been necessary to raise the struggle to a far higher level in order to succeed. Was this impossible? Whether this was so or not, 'there was a certain wavering' (*cf.* interviews with militants) following this first 'victory–failure'. As the renewal programme advanced and expulsion orders were issued, rehousing took priority over all other considerations. Since it was impossible to envisage a collective solution within the framework of the renewal programme, the tenants' association was reduced to an intermediary and advisory role throughout a whole series of individualist and divided negotiations which, apparently, resulted in the rehousing of a good number of the expelled residents: some of them in the H.L.M. dwellings constructed in the programme, some elsewhere in Paris, others still in the suburbs. In all cases, however, the rehousing took place on an individual basis, with or without the association's backing and without any over-all rejection of expulsion, since 'one can't defend slums'. Most of the association's militants were rehoused and the new militants, in 1968–70, were drawn, for the most part, from among new arrivals to the large H.L.M. complex; the demands of the latter were fairly specific and not at all connected with the expulsion problem.

Following this filtering and rehousing process and when the bulk of the renewal programme was already under way, there remained, in *Square Gaieté*, a rump of people who had not left, either because they were unable to, because they did not feel directly threatened, or because they were determined to 'profit' as long as possible from the low rents they were paying, even at the risk of having to find alternative housing in a hurry if they were forcibly expelled by the authorities.

On to this rump, of which the *Impasse Philippe* was a typical example, was grafted a new mobilisatory intervention at the moment when the tenants' association backed out of the affair.

Behind this intervention there was a group of students in one of the faculties who, in the context of agitation at the university, decided to work systematically on the *Cité-du-Peuple*, attempting simultaneously to grasp a social situation in concrete terms, and to set in motion a political process that would involve the inhabitants of these areas. Street agitation and speeches in the market denouncing the promoters' control over the renewal programme marked the movement's search for a point of contact. The students thought they had found it in the defence of residents then under threat of forced eviction. They carried out an inquiry, discovering that the most dramatic case was that of the *concierges*, who did not qualify for rehousing. The renewal agency was no philanthropist; when there was no legal obstacle, it resorted to sheer force. To protest against this, the students occupied the offices of the renewal agency. The police intervened, but there were no arrests. The *concierges* were, however, temporarily rehoused in a near-by building.

Based on the response to this initiative throughout the area (in general it was well received, since the *concierges'* affair was considered a scandal), the students undertook a systematic campaign, especially in an ecologically well-delimited unit, the *Impasse Philippe*, bordering on the sites under renewal and which still contained a few dozen families directly threatened with expulsion. When the letters arrived, warning the residents of impending expulsion procedures, the Action Committee intervened, sticking posters on the walls of the *Impasse* and a door-to-door campaign was carried out, soliciting signatures for a collective petition requesting information from the renewal agency concerning the date and form of eviction/rehousing.

> We made this proposition because we had noticed that the one preoccupation of all the inhabitants of the *Impasse* was, precisely, to know just how the renewal agency planned to deal with them [*à quelle sauce l'organisme rénovateur voulait les manger*] and the latter had left them in total ignorance, so as to make them more ready to accept whatever was offered them, but something on which they could count (Internal Report of Action Committee).

Meanwhile, the agency sent a letter to each of the tenants, making a certain number of very circumstantial propositions, specific to each case. The individualisation of the problem provoked some disinterest in relation to the collective letter, which was signed by only ten tenants who, moreover, were never able to meet together. With each household dealing with its problem separately, the Action Committee lost contact and its activities were finally diluted. A direct and systematic survey carried out among tenants in the *Impasse* who remained there three months later reveals practically no trace of this intervention, neither in the tenants' memories nor in their practice, other than in stray remarks referring to 'some Leftists I kicked out'.

A variety of circumstantial elements may, in part, explain the collapse of this action: the fact that the Action Committee came from outside the area, amateurishness, and lack of regular hours of attendance. More important, however, is the fact that the students arrived at the end of the process, when the game was up and the most militant residents had already left; the base was weak and the operation was at its culminating stage. All the same, it might just as well have been argued that this was the right moment to organise a new style of resistance to expulsion and, in fact, what seems characteristic to us is the existence of very concrete demands and an institutional style of action on the part of the tenants (petition, etc.) together with the appearance of overtly ideological language and spectacular side-shows. There was, in fact, oscillation, but no junction, between the outburst against the injustice and the protest campaign within the framework of the law as carried on by the tenants' association previously.

It must be remembered that the Action Committee had no local roots, and that the residents had tended to individualise their problem following a protest action based on limited objectives. This juxtaposed with a minority ideological protest exposed it by its very logic to repression and, finally, to indifference. The total collapse of the Action Committee was relatively logical.

What is left at the *Impasse Philippe* – old people, the blind who know nothing but this street shortly to be demolished, large families about to move into transit housing facilities, owners trying to squeeze the last drop of profit out of their property – all this belongs to another world, the world of deportation, the reverse face of the new Paris.

Protest from the Bottom: Claims and the Mass Line at Presqu'île

While the same in general terms, the affair here was more dramatic. First, the population is marked by a clear predominance of semi-skilled and unskilled workers, immigrant labourers and ethnic communities. On the other hand, the condition of dwellings here was far more run-down than in the *Cité-du-Peuple* as a whole (*cf.* Table 3). And yet the renewal programme was a good deal less advanced than in the *Square Gaieté*. Was this due to greater population resistance? In part, this was so, since this sector had been a spearhead for the protest struggle throughout the *Cité-du-Peuple* over a period of several years and since, moreover, a committee of badly housed families had been formed in the sector, linked to the tenants' association but focused on the specificity of the situation in the area which consisted in a fusion of measures towards protection against expulsion and the demand for decent housing. Here, the renewal programme was viewed not unfavourably, *provided it was beneficial to the inhabitants,* in terms of the interpretation of the base made up of very low social strata, particularly sensitive to the kind of discriminatory practices liable to be used against them in an environment over which they have no control. The

appropriate demand, then, was that for a multiple-stage operation
with special arrangements (rehousing, for example, of part of the
population elsewhere in the *arrondissement* if it were not possible to
achieve this on the site, construction of a home for the aged, etc.).
There was a very intense mobilisation of some of the inhabitants
around this objective (immigrants and ethnic communities such as
the North African Jews remaining outside). Meetings took place over
a long period of time, inhabitants successfully resisted expulsion
threats (such as the old woman who lived for a year in the still remaining part of a house, under the debris of a construction site, until she
was rehoused!) and petitions received huge numbers of signatures
(700 signatures in one morning). Delegations presented these demands to the City Council and to the *Préfecture*; but the reply was to
come from the O.H.L.M. on the one hand, and from the renewal
agency on the other. The former claimed that it had no legal authority
to give preference to the inhabitants of *Presqu'île* in order to rehouse
them in the *arrondissement*. For the renewal agency, there was no alternative but rehousing elsewhere. For the site itself, the over-all plan allowed for only 135 H.L.M. dwellings. This was all that was obtained
following this mobilisation, even though 2500 dwellings would have to
be replaced. However, at one moment it had been far from certain
that the 135 H.L.M. dwellings would be built, since they were not at
the top of the list of priorities. Furthermore, on the plans these dwellings were located on the site of the present chapel, whose demolition
was being opposed by the Archbishopric. There is a whiff of Machia-
vellianism about this aspect of the over-all plan. It provoked a re-
ligious split in the committee, the lay majority preferring to accept
this promise rather than nothing at all, while the Catholic minority
refused to fight for the demolition of the chapel, which in the renewal
time-table was indispensable prior to the carrying out of this mini-
operation in stages.

Confrontation was inevitable, the inhabitants determined to stay,
in the first phase, while the renewal agency did its utmost to reduce
the only serious localised resistance in the entire *arrondissement*.

There is no point in detailing the intimidatory measures employed:
windows walled-up as soon as a departure had been secured, frequent
robberies (or attempted robberies), poor maintenance of streets and
irregular garbage collection (except in the face of energetic demands),
intimations concerning the growing difficulty of finding satisfactory
alternative housing, etc. Above all, the renewal agency devised the

segmentation of the operation in such a way as to fragment opposition by spreading out the operation in time and space.

The conflict was too sharp for the demands to be imposed with ease. Despite the multiplicity of institutional approaches, on this occasion, this type of action did not carry the necessary weight. The report of the tenants' association made in June 1970, regarding the final interviews with the responsible authorities, is the account of a failure. Apart from a hostel with eighty rooms and the 135 H.L.M. dwellings promised at the outset, nothing was obtained.

The exodus began and, in a few months more than 1000 homes were left empty as a result of individual arrangements, sometimes negotiated with the moral and legal support of the committee, but always from an unfavourable negotiating position. Those who remained behind are those who, on the one hand, do not consider themselves to be in immediate danger (this concerns that part of the area which belongs to the second phase of the operation); the other category remaining is that of the few militants, including those who were unable to leave and whose problem is reaching desperation point. A representative example of the latter is provided by the account of a visit we made: 'The head of the Committee, a devoted militant, very well established in the *quartier*, admits to being discouraged on the local level, while still launching fights in the *arrondissement* as a whole' (visit to a boarding-house, 10 November 1970).

A new type of intervention is growing up in these conditions and in the desperation arising out of them; the most significant example of this is the evolution of the struggle in one of the zones of *Presqu'île, rue de la Boue*.

Rue de la Boue is a slum inhabited, for the most part, by unskilled workers and North African Jews. The committee of badly housed families was not well established there, largely due to cultural barriers; and yet housing conditions were worse than anywhere else, especially since there was a great risk of collapse, and health conditions were well below minimum standards (large numbers of rats, for example). The inhabitants were, moreover, threatened with expulsion. They wanted to leave; how could they not, living in such conditions for ten, fifteen or even twenty years? Yet, with the exception of a very few cases, they refused to leave under just any conditions. They wanted to remain in Paris and, in the case of the Jewish community, they wanted to stay together. Originating from Tunisia, these Jews insisted on staying in an area where they could work and live among

Jews (the employers belonging, for the most part, to the Ashkenazi community, established in the area since the 1930s) and where they could preserve links with the group. Their financial means, however, were extremely limited and they were in less of a position than anyone else to reject the suburbs – and still they remained. Like the aged, the families of Yugoslav labourers, like the large families and the handicapped semi-skilled workers, living crowded together, they were refused rehousing in H.L.M. dwellings because the administrative inquiry showed that 'they are not clean'.

In this situation a new organisation intervened, directly centred on political protest, and which presented itself as such to the inhabitants. Composed of young workers and proletarianised students living in the area, it laboured, above all, to establish a day-to-day relationship with the inhabitants. For example, they helped carry out repairs, they organised games for the children – who were to be the best propagandists for the committee – they proposed to improve a muddy no man's land in order to turn it into a sports field. On the basis of this contact, maintained through ceaseless door-to-door calls and through their daily presence, they organised a Defence Committee for the tenants whose aim was to obtain *rehousing in the same area at reasonable rents*. Meanwhile, they suggested that the inhabitants carry out repairs, install facilities in a nearby area (they occupied a square, and tried to organise a day nursery), and that they resist expulsions and attempts at intimidation. They immediately linked this kind of demand to the general political struggle.

The renewal agency forced the pace in the *rue de la Boue*. They allowed squatters to install themselves in the empty apartments – newly arrived Yugoslav workers whose presence terrified the neighbours. One fine day, a team arrived to cut off the water. There was a general mobilisation. The militants, as well as all the housewives, were there and the children alerted the whole neighbourhood. The water was not cut off after all. The police decided not to intervene.

Interviews with tenants showed the support and sympathy the members of the committee enjoyed, 'despite' their overtly expressed political ties. If the people did not completely join in with the committee's activities, they felt backed up by its action, in the midst of general abandonment and hostility on the part of the public authorities and administrative services with which they have had to deal.

But the committee's demand (*renewal for the benefit of the inhabitants of the area*) was out of proportion to the localised resistance thus constituted. Little by little, energies were dissipated over this point. A meeting called to discuss ways of stimulating renewal action (approved by the tenants in the course of door-to-door visits) collapsed through poor attendance. Children were directly threatened by the police ('You'll spend your whole life in jail if you play with those people there'). Some partial collapses produced a general mood of anxiety. The rate of departures speeded up and, for the short term, it is inevitable that rehousing will be in accordance with individual formulae (controlled by the renewal agency).

The militants knew it. But, for them, there was never any question of their winning a protest battle whose magnitude clearly exceeded their strength: 'The main thing is, things have changed in people's minds.' The failure of a protest, then, results in a political radicalisation. Is this really so? For the committee, consequently, it now became necessary to generalise the struggle throughout the *Cité-du-Peuple* and to broaden its action.

A demonstration was held in the market, with placards, posters and speeches; the process had begun again. Meanwhile, the phases of the renewal programme were forging ahead, without any great modification in the original projects. The political struggle, in the strict sense of the term, had once more gained the upper hand.

The Fight for Rehousing as a Social Process

If this account, based on the principal protest actions, has, on occasion, revealed a certain logic, it is none the less clear that we cannot substitute the description of a mechanism for an explanation of its operation. Our aim being more to identify the conditions for the emergence of social movements in the 'urban' field than to concentrate on a given conjuncture, we shall attempt to establish, summarily, the principal components of each of these actions (or of all the actions together, linked around an objective and a mode of intervention) and to determine their interrelations, especially in terms of the type of impact produced on the urban structure and on the current state of social relations.

In Table 4, we shall advance (with all the requisite precautions) a semi-theoretical, semi-descriptive classification of the components of each action.

We are not in a position systematically to interpret the connections

TABLE 4 *Analysis of the fight for rehousing in the Cité-du-Peuple*

Areas	Issues	Social base	Type of organisation	Social force
Square Gaieté	Promoters' profit Renewal programme Rehousing of residents	Multi-class, High proportion of artisans and shopkeepers	Tenants' association: demand-orientated, national in scope, but strongly established locally	Workers with shopkeepers' support
Presqu'ile	As in *Square Gaieté* Lack of repairs Bad housing conditions	Predominance of semi- and unskilled workers, immigrants and foreigners	As in *Square Gaieté*	Unqualified workers
Impasse Philippe	As in *Square Gaieté*	Compared to *Square Gaieté:* more working class and older population, more immigrants	Action committee from outside area linking economic demands to ideological protest	Students from outside area
Rue de la Boue	As in *Presqu'ile*	Predominance of Jews, North Africans and unskilled workers	Local action committee linking economic demands to political and ideological protest	Community and proletarianised students living in area

Opponents	Demands	Actions	Urban impact and political impact
Paris City Council *Préfecture* O.H.L.M. Mixed renewal agency	Construction of H.L.M. dwellings Rehousing	Propaganda Petitions Delegations Meetings Street demonstrations	(1) Construction of H.L.M. dwellings without rehousing resident population (2) Rehousing of a portion of the population individually negotiated (3) Remans a hard core to be expelled (4) Demobilisation
Paris City Council *Préfecture* O.H.L.M. Renewal agency	As in *Square Gaieté* Multiple-stage operation	As in *Square Gaieté* Non-departure of tenants Frequent meetings Regular hours of attendance	(1) As in *Square Gaieté* (2) As in *Square Gaieté* (3) 135 H.L.M. dwellings promised to rehouse a portion of the population in the area (4) A major portion yet to be rehoused (5) Discouragement, but continuation of intervention
Mixed renewal agency	Rehousing in area at same rents Resistance to expulsion	Occupation of renewal agency's offices (confrontation with police) Agitation and propaganda Petition to be signed by tenants	(1) Imposed provisional rehousing of one couple (2) Rejection of collective petition by most residents (3) Withdrawal, followed by extinction of Action Committee after ten months of existence (4) 'Every man for himself' among remaining households
Mixed renewal agency	Provision of facilities in area Rehousing in equivalent dwelling close to place of work Resistance to expulsion	Agitation Daily community self-help Collective resistance to water-cuts Petition	(1) Renewal agency backs down concerning expulsion time limits (2) In the short term: eviction (3) Population support for resistance to expulsion (4) A certain political radicalisation

which emerge from this schema. We lack too many connecting links. We can, however, extract some of these, first *analytically* between the different elements, and then *synthetically* by reconstructing the logic of a particular action.

Relations between the elements in a protest action

(i) The more a *general issue* (the threat of expulsion) is backed by a *specific issue* (housing conditions), the tougher the confrontation and the more intense the mobilisation (*Impasse Philippe*). The *social force* mobilised is always a *specification* of the *social base* but they do not coincide. This specification is directly provided by the type of *organisation* and, consequently, by the demands put forward. Relationship between the *social base* and the type of *organisation*.

(ii) The more *working class* the base, and the more it is ethnically French, the stronger the local roots of the national interest-group organisation (*e.g.* tenants' association).

(iii) The lower the social strata of the base, the easier it is for a revolutionary movement to take root politically (the *sine qua non* being that it is locally based).

(iv) Any external intervention remains separated from the social base.

(v) The more the adversary is diversified and global, the more chance there is that some demands will be successful.

(vi) But chances do not vary in terms of demands relative to the renewal programme. Let us say, rather, that the chances of success rise as the *demands deviate* from the programme.

(vii) The greater the correspondence between the immediate interests of the social base and the *demand*, the greater the *intensity* of the action. This correspondence, which is the result of organisation, should be understood in the sense of an immediate *material* response to the material situation which lies at its origin.

(viii) The *urban* impact depends directly on the issue and on the *level of mobilisation*. The mechanism is summarised in Table 5.

(ix) The political impact depends on the *urban* impact, on the level of *mobilisation* and on the *type of organisation*. We can analyse the relationship between the elements according to that shown in Table 6.

The social determination of actions

We are faced with four actions which we shall deal with in the same order as in Table 4.

(i) In the *first case*, the social base, organisation, level of mobilisation and demand are compatible, but the resulting political confrontation

TABLE 5 *Urban impact: relationship between level of issues and level of mobilisation*

Level of issues*	Level of mobilisation	
	High	Low
High	Political confrontation	Demand defeat
Low	Demand victory	*Status quo*
		Public assistance

* High/low on this dimension denotes the extent to which the urban structure is brought into question (*e.g.* high = the whole renewal programme).

TABLE 6 *Political impact: relationship between urban impact, level of mobilisation and type of organisation*

	Level of mobilisation	Type of organisation	Political impact
	High	Demand-focused	Continuation of demand-focused action
		Political	Direct link between demand-orientation and political struggle
Won	Low	Demand-focused	Social integration (paternalism)
		Political	Political disaggregation (politico–institutional integration)
Outcome of demand action	High	Demand-focused	Discouragement, demobilisation
		Political	Political radicalisation
Lost	Low	Demand-focused	
			Individual withdrawal
		Political	

was *deviated* (transformed demand) and, consequently, there was a gap between the final demand and the initial issue which led to demobilisation.

(ii) In the *second case*, there was a constant correspondence which resulted in a *defeat* due to the limits of a purely demand-focused mobilisation.

(iii) In the *third case*, besides the particularly unfavourable conjuncture, the type of organisation – external to the social base and without local roots – seems to have conditioned the *non-fusion* of elements which characterises this unsuccessful action.

(iv) Finally, in the *fourth case*, there was a correspondence between the social base, organisation and demands, but the process seems to have ended in a defeat for the demands (due to the prevailing power relations) which could result in a political radicalisation.

Conclusion: the Interaction between Urban Renewal and Social Movements

The results of two other surveys carried out in two large renewal sectors, as well as a fourth concerning an *arrondissement* in which the renewal is being carried out entirely by private bodies, point in the general direction of the observations we have laid out.

Only the demand for multiple-stage operations, claiming rehousing of the population in the same area at reasonable rents, makes it possible to probe the *social base* and the *social strength* and thus to create the conditions for success. But this demand, which leads to no change in the social content of the Paris area, runs directly counter to the direction of the renewal programme such as we have established it. The issue, consequently, being of great importance, the fight becomes considerably tougher and everything depends on the prevailing power relations, these being largely a function of the linking of the urban demand-focused organisations with the political process.

If the national-scale tenants' association is sufficiently powerful for it to be able to attempt a long-term battle (it has already done so in certain cases) its means are very limited in the case of Paris because of the capital's lack of administrative autonomy and of the unconditional support afforded by the majority in the Paris Council. With barely any means of action within the institutional system, there remain only agitation and mass demand-focused movements (*e.g.* demonstrations, resistance to expulsions, etc.) which would lead the tenants' association along a path forbidden to it by the declaration in its statutes of non-involvement in politics.

On the other hand, the only movements ready to engage in agitation on such a level are poorly established in the population, which forces them into a very long detour, by way of the defence (demand-orientated and legal) of the inhabitants. These militant groups are, however, above all concerned with specifically political action giving priority to other battlefronts. Their fight remains, then, at the level of arousing consciousness, over a limited period, among the inhabitants of the area, but without stirring up long-term mass resistance to the renewal programme.

The characteristics of the programme, concentrating in itself the expression of urban policy in respect of the capital, constitute such an issue that it weighs heavily, as indicated, on the formation and orientation of urban social movements in the various areas of Paris.

Conversely, the impotence of these movements in relation to the programme's stated objectives (which, at best, they may manage to delay) could permit the deployment of the renewal programme according to its own logic with, here and there, experiments in political radicalisation in certain sectors of the population committed to an unequal struggle. If the demand-focused movement were to become strengthened (this is now happening in two areas) we would probably see two immediate consequences upon the content of the renewal programme:

(1) the ideological envelope of the new urban forms would become more 'social' and less overtly segregationist and technocratic;
(2) above all, the process of handing over to the private sector would be slowed down, because the administrative authorities would offer an element of guarantee that the programme would be faithfully carried out.

A real alteration in the current programme (*e.g.* in the direction of low-rent housing or public facilities) seems to require a prior and complete transformation of the elements of the problem.

Such an outcome does not signify the failure of the nascent urban social movements in the Paris region; it is a matter, rather, of a shift in the centres of conflict (*e.g.* towards the problem of transport) and, above all, of the social necessity of their linkage with the general political process.

Thus urban issues become political issues and the struggle for the environment includes and specifies the class struggle.

Chapter 6

The Social Prerequisites for the Upheaval of Urban Social Movements: an Exploratory Study of the Paris Metropolitan Area, 1968–73

Introduction

Urban contradictions are increasingly finding themselves at the centre of the social and political stakes of advanced capitalist societies; this is for two basic reasons:

(i) The first refers to the essential role played by the consumption process in advanced capitalism. The growing socialisation of consumption and the intervention of the state in its management, both of which underlie the urban problematic, are key elements in the organisation of consumption in that they deepen contradictions while politicising them.

(ii) The second relates to the diffusion of an urban ideology as an ideological form specific to the dominant classes. This ideology 'naturalises' class contradictions by considering them as 'urban'. It does this by encapsulating class differences into one humanist totality and by preaching the social causality of spatial forms.

In France, the current interest in urban problems is not due to popular struggles or to the initiatives taken by the trade unions and political organisations of the dominated classes. On the contrary, the increased visibility of urban struggles is the result of the emphasis by the dominant classes on the urban theme. In fact, there has been in the last few years no particular increase of urban struggles in France, although popular movements centred around consumption had already accompanied the capitalist industrialisation process. The Commune had been more characterised by these themes than the movement of May 1968.

Yet we are willing to make the historical and theoretical wager that there will be a significant development of urban social movements as a means of changing social relations, and this will arise from urban contradictions. Underlying such a hypothesis are more general observations as to the way new structural contradictions are made visible by social practice, for it is the dominant classes which usually have at their disposal the experience and knowledge enabling them to discover historical tendencies and to define them according to their own terms, while the dominated classes feel the effects; but, consciousness evading them, they can only act defensively until a social movement is constituted expressing the fusion of consciousness and experience, solidarity in struggle. For example, during the rise of the European labour movement, the 'social question' had first been posed by the reformist bourgeoisie (as in Proudhonian populism) and had to a certain extent helped to constitute it. In the same way, the contemporary 'urban question', raised by the technocratic elites, has its roots in the structural contradictions of the present phase of the capitalist mode of production. But while the dominant ideology deforms these contradictions, it also arouses the popular masses by reminding them of the exploitation and oppression characterising our societies. In making this analogy we are not proposing the replacement of the labour/capital contradiction which defines the working class by a new principal contradiction defined in the sphere of socialised consumption; rather, it is the deepening of a secondary structural contradiction and the new historical role it can play through social movements and the processes of change that it can potentially provoke.

In order to explore this major hypothesis, it is necessary to carry out two types of research at the same time: first, one addressed to the structural evolution of capitalism, the place of socialised consumption and state intervention, and the articulation of these historical characteristics to what are identified as 'urban problems'; second, one must investigate political and protest movements arising out of urban contradictions, in order to understand their impact on social relations and the political class struggle in particular.

As much of our other works have focused on a structural analysis,[1] we would have liked to present some exploratory results and initial interpretations of a systematic study of urban social movements in the Paris region.[2] However, it must be emphasised that the distinction between structure and practice is only an analytical one, and that concrete research must closely articulate the two, precisely in order to understand their interaction. This has been the theoretical principle underlying our research into urban social movements; it has been through understanding the structural nature of unfolding social practices, through studying their impacts on the so-called 'structures', that we have been able to arrive at an 'objective analysis of subjective practices' and at an explanation by the subjects of these 'objects', which are crystallised social relations.

The purpose of the research presented here is *to study the social conditions of emergence, of dominated class practices, which, arising out of urban contradictions, directly or indirectly transform social relations against the dominant structural logic.* We first direct our attention to urban protest movements, and it is from our observation of them as historical practices that we can identify the conditions and components susceptible of transforming them into social movements; i.e. while we recognise the non-emergence of urban social movements in the historical conjuncture studied, we aim to identify the conditions of emergence of certain elements which precede their development. We shall present the research in order to assess the major results and enlarge our problematic to include the question of the relationships between politics, the state and urban social movements.

Elements of Theory and Method for the Study of Urban Social Movements

From a differential study of urban protest movements we are attempting to establish their potential for changing the social relations contained within them. To do this we put forward the hypothesis that a collective action is characterised at one and the same time by the structural stake to which it relates, by the social position of the actors concerned, and by the forms the action take. Moreover, it is defined by its effects on social structure, i.e. the urban system, political relations and ideological structures. In addition, as any other social process, it unfolds through the contradictory dialectic of dominant and dominated classes, this implying a double classification of variables in relation to social *ensembles*: class situation, social force, type of organisation, type of protest and forms of action. Finally, in practice, every analysis of the variations observed implies the theoretical predefinition of the scale of variation, according to the questions which underlie the research. Typologies have therefore been constructed for each of the variables thus defined, and this is the case not only for the dominated classes but for the dominant classes as well.

The analysis consists of the classification within a theoretical framework of observed urban struggles, the unit of observation being each struggle. From this classification we have attempted to give an account of the regularities observed in the covariation of the typologies in relation to a statistical treatment of observed struggles.

Our research is based on urban struggles in the Paris region which have occurred since 1968. We first carried out a pilot study on 180 struggles which were related to different issues. From the general tendencies which were established, we selected three issues which became the object of the in-depth study: housing, transport and the environment. Between 1972 and 1974 we focused our study on protest movements in the *grands ensembles* of the Paris region and on the squatting movement. For 1975–6, a study of transport was carried out. Research is planned in 1977–8 on the ecological movement and on environmental defence.[3]

We are here presenting the results of the analysis of the general tendencies in urban struggles which have been observed in the 180 movements which took place between 1968 (a significant historical watershed) and 1973 (the date of the start of the research). Our selection of the struggles observed is not haphazard: all were socially visible and had sufficient information to enable them to be classified into a framework. The major source of information was obtained by a systematic analysis of newspapers and weeklies, as well as the pamphlets, documents and dossiers of unions and political organisations. In many cases field work supplemented our information. It is evident that Paris is atypical because of the visibility of the struggles, and while we cannot say that our sample is representative we can nevertheless:

(i) consider that these struggles have the most general scope, which is our object of study; and

(ii) argue on the basis of the relationship inside an historically defined whole, the purpose being to determine what elements can lead to significant social effects.

As to the research method, we must emphasise three fundamental points:

(i) the theoretical framework is the basic means of classification;

(ii) the classification of each struggle in the framework's typology is qualitative, though it rests upon series of pre-constructed indicators – It is more important to have coherent criteria for each struggle than to assert the perfect pertinence of all classifications, for in understanding all the relations internal consistency is paramount;

(iii) covariations were obtained by the direct comparison of frequencies in the cross-analysis two by two of variables, i.e. we are here concerned with tendencies whose validity can be justified only within the framework of a pilot study.

Despite the relative degree of formality of our presentation, one should really not give it more credit than one would to a classical descriptive and historical study. The use of variables is simply to organise our analysis and should not be seen as classical procedures for the analysis of causality. This is why it is important to use the tendencies observed as simply the basis for reflection, which should later be verified in the in-depth phases of our research. Still, we would like here to present our exploratory results and, from the onset, base on concrete observation our general reflection upon the progressive formation of urban social movements.

Research Results: the Principal Tendencies of the Social Mechanisms underlying Urban Struggles in the Paris Region

We have studied the interactions between elements making up urban struggles, as well as the significant combinations producing different types of urban effects. We shall summarise the principal results by showing, on the one hand, the social logic of the production of these effects, and on the other, prior to this, the principal types of urban social movements which appear to us to synthesise the regularity of the relations between the different elements.

Towards a Typology of the Processes of Urban Struggle

Observations made on the determination of the elements making up a process of urban struggle can be organised in a way which can establish certain typical profiles of relationships between the different elements. The purpose of such an undertaking is to synthesise the information we have on protest movements. We must point out, however, that such a typology is not in itself explanatory, and this means that it will be necessary to examine the effects of each of these types on the social practices to which they give rise.

We can see emerging three kinds of processes in which type of organisation is clearly a pivotal element, but where the different elements have autonomous effects which organise themselves independently of the effect produced by the organisation variable:

(1) A process of economic protest, based upon a predominantly working-class economic organisation constituting a social force centred around immediate demands related to the reproduction of the labour force, more often than not, to housing and urban policy. It is strongly mobilised and sets up a relation of force which leads to a divided attitude on the part of the dominant classes; the nature of the demands will predispose them to *laissez-faire* policies, but the level of mobilisation will incite them to repression. This first type of process, which has a strong internal coherence, also appears to be the most prevalent type of urban social movement and is close to what one could call a *trade-unionism of collective consumption*.

(2) A process of political protest, based around a multi-class political organisation also constituting a social force; but while it is also centred around demands related to the reproduction of the labour force, it places them at the level of a reorganisation of the urban system, as is the case for the issue of *transport*, which is generally associated with this type of process. While this type generally achieves only a medium level of mobilisation through the creation of a certain level of force, it is subject to frequent repression, not only because of its level of mobilisation, but also because of the demands put forward, even though its multi-class social base protects it somewhat from repressive intervention. Despite its strong protest base, this process could be qualified in terms of an *urban political movement* to the extent that it attempts to question the logic of the urban system, without, however, prejudging its objective effect in what concerns class relations.

(3) This last type appears to be structured around an ideological organisation, instigated both by a student social force and by an issue which attributes an important place to the problematic of the environment. What largely determines the type of protests which characterises it are social relations and a generally low level of mobilisation.

As long as the level of mobilisation is low and the type of organisation is not threatening, the dominant classes will hesitate to intervene; on the other hand, the type of organisation and its social force usually provoke the anger of the authorities. Because of the ambiguity of its situation and the reactions it provokes, this type could justifiably be characterised as an *ideological urban movement*. The highly differentiated forms and effects in relation to the articulations of an ideological practice, and its displacement *vis-à-vis* protest and political practices, make its development still highly uncertain.

Having characterised processes of urban struggle in this way, their significance as social practices can only be deduced from the observation of their effects on class relations and on the urban system.

The Social Production by Urban Struggles of Ideological and Political Urban Effects

As was noted before, by the term 'effect of an urban struggle' we mean the impact produced by a process of struggle on social relations, and this according to a triple dimension: the urban system as a specific organisation of economic relations at the level of the reproduction of the labour force; class political relations; and class ideological relations. If we are to go beyond a purely internal characterisation of the process, we must study the production of these effects in order to understand the role of urban struggles as social practices. Their social definition will be given by the evidence they produce in the social structures from which they arise. It is by relating the characteristics of the elements constituting the process to their effects that we will be able to establish the dialectic between social practices and the structured relations which underlie them.

The production of urban effects

We will differentiate between effect on an urban struggle (its satisfaction or non-satisfaction) and effect on the urban system as a whole, according to our theoretical categorisation of urban effects, which we will not repeat here.

Table 7 indicates the variables characteristic of a process of struggle which positively relate to the satisfaction or non-satisfaction of a protest; it is especially with regards to the latter that obstacles to the satisfaction of a protest are more evident.

TABLE 7

Variables determining the non-satisfaction of a protest	Variables determining the satisfaction of a protest
A political urban issue	Immediate protest
A social base with a large proportion of single persons	A form of class struggle dominated by *pressure type*
A social base with a large proportion of immigrants	

A dominant-class situation, represented by
    the state apparatus
    public capital, or
    the state-domination apparatus	

The importance of *students* in the social force	
The intervention of the state apparatus as social force for the dominant classes	
The intervention for the dominated classes of a *political organisation*	
For the dominated classes, the articulation of the protest movement to a political practice	
The expression of a *reorganisation type of protest*	
The form of dominated-class struggles on the basis of the creation of a relation of forces	
Repression of the dominant classes	

From these observations, one can put forward the hypothesis that the non-satisfaction of urban protest is essentially linked to the politicisation of the stake. This entails, on the one hand, the intervention of the state on behalf of the dominant classes (either at the level of the stake itself, or because of the presence of the state apparatus or public capital in the class situation, or even because of the intervention of the state apparatus as a social force), and, on the other hand, it also entails the intervention of a political organisation, or an articulation with political practice, for the dominated classes.

This main effect is reinforced by the difficulty of satisfying a reorganisational-type protest (contrary to what happens in the case of immediate protest) and by the vulnerability of certain social groups (immigrants, single persons, students). This negative influence on satisfaction is expressed through the forms of struggle: a *pressure type* of action tends to have a positive influence, but this can become negative when the intervention attempts to create a relation of force which must generally confront the repression of the dominant classes.

Therefore, there does appear to be a fairly clear attempt to prevent any politicisation of urban struggles, and if this happens, due to the initiative of the state or the dominated classes, it negatively affects struggles at the level of protest. This would imply that on the whole urban struggles are largely determined according to whether the dominant classes give a *political* status to the contradiction, i.e. whether they see it at the level of their interests as a whole. The outcome of a struggle will now depend, in the conjuncture considered, on whether it will become autonomous, or whether it will become part of the political process, and hence the importance for union and political organisations to control the dialectic between narrow corporatism and an excess of politicisation which undermines their popular basis.

While there appear to be few regularities in the determination of regulatory effects, this analysis is strengthened by the observation of determinants which produce effects of *urban restructuration* on the urban system. If we examine the linkages presented in Table 8, we can discover that the effects of reproduction of the urban system are directly linked to the intervention of political variables in the process of struggle. The effect is almost systematic and appears more or less to follow the sequence illustrated in Figure 3. This again appears to be confirmed by the difference between the effects produced by the 'urban-political' issue and those produced by the 'housing' issue, the latter being the most removed from a direct political relationship.

Therefore, one way or another, the more political a struggle becomes, the more urban effects remain inside the logic of the pre-existing urban organisation.

This result would lead us to conclude that the *politicisation of a struggle does not increase its efficiency at the urban level.* Would this mean that the dominant classes are unable to tolerate the politicisation of urban contradictions as soon as they attempt to go beyond the stage of reproduction? Or, are we really confronted by a conjunctural effect in which the political intervention of the dominated classes is too weak at the level of urban protest movements to threaten existing relations of force? Or could it even be that the dominant classes themselves are taking political initiatives which are so important that they cannot tolerate any other protest or regulation of the urban system?

We cannot, on the basis of this preliminary data, give a definitive answer to a question so important for the characterisation of urban struggles, for this could lead us to a hypothesis with heavy consequences – if such effects were to be confirmed, if the politicisation and efficiency of the struggle were to be disjointed by the repressive intervention of the dominant classes, one could hypothesise that the subversive potential of urban struggle would become intolerable to them. But we will not develop this hypothesis and we will limit ourselves to a confirmation of the tendency and to raising some of the questions it implies.

The production of political effects

A distinction has been made between two types of political effects: in the conjuncture resulting from the outcome of a struggle, effects on class relations of force; using the organisation of the dominated classes in the struggle as an indicator, the effect on the accumulated political strength of the classes present. Tables 9 and 10 can help us establish the significant links between the variables of a process of struggle and the political effects, from which we can isolate a number of very clear trends.

If one closely examines the variables conditioning each effect of urban struggle upon class political relations, it appears to be the result of a double permutation: when the stake which is essentially economic for the dominant classes becomes political for the dominated classes, the latter have the advantage; conversely, when the dominant classes politicise the problem, while the dominated classes remain at the level of urban protest, relations of force will be in favour

TABLE 8

Determinant variables of a reproduction effect on the urban system	*Determinant variables of a regulatory effect on the urban system*
Urban political stakes	The housing stake
The class situation of the dominant classes, characterised by: the state apparatus, or the state-domination apparatus, or public capital	
The state apparatus constituted as social force of the dominant classes	
For the dominated classes, articulation to a political organisation	
For the dominated classes, articulation to a political practice	
For the dominated classes, the creation of a relation of force	
Repression of the dominant classes	

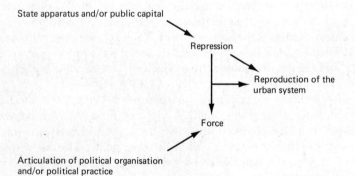

FIGURE 3

TABLE 9

Variables determining a relation of force favourable to the dominated classes	Variables determining a relation of force favourable to the dominant classes
The housing stake	The urban-political stake
A predominantly French social base	The transport stake
Capital as a social force of the dominant classes	State apparatus and/or public capital intervention
Articulation to the political organisation of the dominated classes	An economic-type organisation for the dominated classes
Protest centred around social relations	Organisation of the dominant classes around a productive enterprise
High level of mobilisation	Low level of mobilisation
The use of *pressure* as a means of struggle	The use of *force* as a means of struggle
	Repression of the dominant classes

TABLE 10

Variables having a positive effect on dominated-class organisation	Variables having a negative effect on dominated-class organisation
The housing stake	The urban-political stake
A predominantly French multi-class situation	A predominantly immigrant social base
Intervention by private capital in particular	A student social force
Intervention by management-centred enterprises	Repression of the dominant classes
Articulation to a dominated-class political organisation	
Intervention of a political organisation	
Protest based on social relations	
Immediate protest	

of the dominant classes.

This will depend on the kind of issue at the basis of the struggle (housing is, for example, more favourable for the dominated classes than urban politics or transport), as well as the relative political weight of the social base (immigrants being in the least advantageous position).

Another determinant of this effect deserves notice: protest centred around social relations tends to create a relation of forces favourable to the dominated classes. This effect is autonomous, for the social-relations type of protest (an ideological organisation with a student social base) does not correlate or correlates negatively with the effect observed. It would therefore appear that political effects favourable to the dominated classes can be achieved only if an economic-type protest is overcome; as a consequence, the processes producing economic and political effects favourable to the dominated classes are largely disjointed. *So while at the level of urban protest, the politicisation of the stake generally determined negative effects for the dominated classes, it was at the level of the relation of political forces that the politicisation of the stake was determinant for them, as was the overcoming of a strictly economic level of protest.*

These tendencies are confirmed by analysis of the other political effects related to the impact of the struggle upon the organisation of the dominated classes. In fact, it can be observed that organisation is strengthened when it is associated or related to a political organisation, particularly in cases when it is centred on the housing stake and confronts a preferably private and management-orientated capital. On the other hand, there can be negative effects for dominated-class organisation when its action has economic elements and the stake is politically charged for the dominant classes.

The influence of these variables on dominated-class organisation is enhanced by two other elements:

(i) The social base and the social force reinforce negative or positive effects according to the possibility of a general social intervention at their disposal. There are more positive effects for a multi-class and predominantly French social base, and conversely effects are more negative for a predominantly immigrant or student social base.

(ii) In addition, protest centred around social relations confirms its positive political effects for the dominated classes, but in the production of its effects it is also accompanied by an immediate type of protest; that is to say, while we have noted the importance of political organisation for the reorganisation of demands usually related to the labour force, we see here a reversal of the effect of this type of protest on the strengthening of dominated-class organisation. The dialectic observed would be more or less as follows: urgent qualitative protests create breaches in the social order which strengthen the political organisation of the dominated classes: an organisation which can then insist, by generalising a particular struggle, on the reorganisation of the whole system.

The production of political effects appears to be largely dependent upon the interaction of three series of variables: the social capacity which the forces present dispose of; the level of protest expressed; and the economic or political involvement of social forces. The more political is this involvement, the better are its chances to tip the scales in its favour at the political level. When the two sides involved are politicised, other variables will determine the outcome, and generally it will be in favour of the dominant classes.

Two things can be learned from these observations and related to a general analysis of urban social movements:

(i) *political effects have a logic of their own which is not cumulative, but, instead, is contradictory with the actual sequence of protest;*

(ii) *political effects are largely determined by the introduction of political elements at the heart of the struggle — By saying this, we deny the possibility of urban struggles developing into political ones solely through their own internal dynamic.*

There can be action on the political front only if there are present in the urban movement elements related to political struggle.

The production of ideological effects
One of the most complex analyses on the social efficiency of urban struggles is that which relates to their impact on the ideology of the actors engaged in a process of struggle. This is not only due to problems of observation but also to the multiplicity of often contradictory sources.

Table 11 summarises the major variables acting upon the two most important ideological groups observed: 'reproduction–integration' and 'contestation–rupture'. One can identify several types of determinants:

(i) The *symbolic* stake relates to a problematic whose ideological content tends towards reproduction, while the *housing* stake is more favourable to contestation. We can here observe a well-known effect, which is the displacement of struggles towards issues abandoned by the dominant ideology – in particular, the environmental theme.

(ii) With regards to class situation, the general social situation is more important than the place in relations of production in determining this effect. Once again families play a major role in ideological reproduction, while the inherent social weakness of immigrants does not allow them to question the social order. On the other hand, students, despite their rather negative effect on the successful outcome of protest action, reveal themselves to be ideological agents *par excellence*. Still, it is important to observe the importance of dominant-class composition in the determination of ideological effects. We find an opposition between state intervention and public capital supporting reproduction, and private-capital intervention supporting contestation. However, while one could believe that ideological revolt in urban contradictions is facilitated by direct contact with the logic of capital, *state intervention in fact acts as a screen which makes the recognition of the structural logic underlying problems difficult*. But state intervention is not unequivocal, for while its integration–regulation branch contributes to ideological reproduction, its function of domination, particularly through the government and the Prefect, is one of the variables which can provoke protest. We cannot therefore juxtapose ideological effects produced by the public with effects produced by the private, *but we can instead talk about an ideological contestation which is defined by the clarity of the class logic of the dominant classes*. This can be at the economic level (private capital) as well as at the political level (domination function of the state).

(iii) One decisive and extremely revealing effect is the intervention of dominated-class organisations in the production of ideology. This reproduction effect is aided by an ideological organisation which does not otherwise articulate itself to any other during the struggle, while the contestation effect is instigated by a political organisation and by other equally political organisations. This element therefore supports the classical thesis in historical materialism, according to which ideological interventions are produced from political interventions, while any attempt to isolate ideological processes, especially by crystallising their autonomy in a separate organisation, will necessarily remain a prisoner of the dominant ideology.

(iv) On another level this last analysis is strengthened by the study

TABLE II

Variables determining an ideological effect of reproduction–integration	Variables determining an ideological effect of contestation–rupture
Symbolic stake	Housing stake
Family-dominated social base	Intervention by capital
Immigrant-dominated social base	Intervention by state apparatus of domination

Intervention in a dominant class situation of
  the state apparatus, or
  public capital, or
  state apparatus of integration–regulation
	A student social force

Intervention of the state apparatus as the social force of the dominant classes	Intervention of a political organisation for the dominated classes
Intervention of an ideological organisation for the dominated classes	Articulation to a political organisation
Non-articulation to another type of organisation	A 'reorganisation-type' protest
Lack of articulation to other struggles	A form of struggle through a relation of force
'Pressure-type' form of dominated-class struggle	A high level of mobilisation
Integration-type intervention by the dominant classes	

of the ideological effect produced by the type of protest, for if one cannot observe a direct effect upon protest centred on social relations, protest centred on reorganisation does create a contestation effect; that is to say, ideology does not summon ideology, and the need for a transformation of social relations does not necessarily lead to a consciousness of this need for change. On the other hand, this effect is attained more easily as soon as protest becomes related to the reorganisation of urban problems, because concrete objectives for changing the logic of the urban system enables the development of a conscious opposition. This can be seen as an additional confirmation of the necessary political mediation in ideological transformation.

(v) Last, forms of struggle produce ideological effects which are congruent with their content: a forceful action with a high level of mobilisation will encourage consciousness, while a pressure type of intervention will be more closely associated with a reproduction effect.

With regards to the dominant classes, while it is logical to observe the influence of an integration tactic, it is also important not to perceive a precise ideological effect associated with repression. This demonstrates the fact that repression does not only have one meaning with regards to the effects produced, and that, moreover, it does not always lead to revolt. However, with regards to the evidence which repression leaves in the consciousness of the subjects, it is modulated by the content and the intensity of the practices which it attempts to counteract.

Social determination of urban, political and ideological effects
If one attempts to identify a few of the most significant traits related to the social determination of the urban, political and ideological effects of urban struggles in the Paris region during the period 1968–73, one can emphasise the following:

(i) It is the political initiative of the dominant classes which largely structures the process, especially in relation to urban effects which, as soon as the stake becomes political, are rarely in the interests of the dominated classes.

(ii) Political effects are derived above all from the discrepancy in the importance (political or economic) attributed to the stake by the social forces present.

(iii) Ideological effects are largely subordinated to the political components of the process: reproduction effect when politicisation is by the dominant classes, contestation effect when organised political intervention is by the dominated classes.

(iv) The interplay of the types of protest upon the effects of the struggle shows the specificity of a protest according to the conjuncture it finds itself in and the stake to which it relates; that is to say, the impact of elements of an urban struggle upon their effects cannot be established in isolation from the whole of the process and from the precise content of each element which is characterised by the conjuncture. This last observation is fundamental from a methodological point of view, for what it means in the concrete is that one cannot identify the general mechanisms of urban struggles in terms of their historical content but only in terms of a transcription of these contents into analytical categories, thus enabling generalisation, i.e. what makes a struggle more or less revolutionary is not so much the content of its protest, or its intensity, but the *ensemble* of effects produced which themselves depend upon a series of variables which change according to the conjuncture. This does not mean that it is impossible to establish general rules, but, simply, that these rules cannot arise directly from observation but must undergo a process of theorisation of concrete practices which can reveal the social relations underlying them.

It is by this approach that we have been able to establish the three major characteristics which are the essence of our observations and analyses on the production of effects:

(i) There is a disjunction between the mechanisms producing urban effects and political and ideological effects favourable to the dominated classes. This goes against a cumulative concept of protest and politico–ideological practices.

(ii) Most of the processes observed are the initiative of the dominant classes, which confine urban struggles to a defensive experience, and consequently make them highly dependent on their localism and discontinuity. This explains why one must insist on the importance of the conjunctural nature of each struggle and also on the evaluation of its effects.

(iii) The production of political and ideological effects supportive of the dominated classes appears, when they directly confront the logic of capital, to be largely determined by their political initiative; but the danger of this approach is that it can also contribute to a distancing from conditions supportive of a protest action. The risk urban struggles run is that of continual oscillation between protest movements, which reproduce the social order, and exemplary political interventions, which are still in the minority. This dilemma cannot probably be overcome within the context of the internal dynamics of urban movements themselves, but only through the place they may progressively come to occupy in political struggles as a whole.

Correlations between urban, political and ideological effects
We already know that the production processes of urban, political and ideological effects are not only very different, but in one instance also contradictory; yet we have attempted to establish

what are the statistical correlations between the different types of effects. This approach appears to be fully justified, as the result is quite surprising: *there appears to be an almost perfect correlation between all the effects which can be considered as being positive from the point of view of the dominated classes*, even though their origins may have been different and the different effects between them were not evident.

A number of points must therefore be made:

(i) A political defeat cannot be compensated by a strong ideological protest, nor can a protest setback be strengthened by political or ideological means. Positive and negative effects correlate, and thus the dissociation which operated at the level of processes converges at the level of effects.

(ii) 'Urban corporatism', which consisted in dissociating the political impact from the protest impact, does not pay; if one wins, it is on all counts. This statement must be reconciled with the preceding result related to the negative effect of the politicisation of struggle on urban protest.

(iii) There is a mutual reinforcement between the relations of political forces supportive of the dominated classes and the positive outcome of the protest movement.

(iv) Ideology gives form to practice, and can thus contest where it has had a concrete experience of successful struggle against the dominant logic.

The significance of these observations is quite considerable, for if one relates them to the determinants of the effects established above, it would mean that *a protest struggle must be kept independent of a political struggle in order to obtain positive urban effects on the one hand and positive political effects on the other; but the two types of processes must be developed (especially the political struggle against the logic of capital) not only so that they can achieve specific goals but also so that they can mutually reinforce each other.*

Such a perspective means that we must attempt, even in a tentative way, an initial synthesis of the observations and analyses made on the general tendencies of urban struggles in the Paris region.

From Urban Struggles to Social Practice: a Few Remarks on the General Tendencies of the Relationship between Processes of Struggle and Structural Effects

Our characterisation of processes of urban struggles has led us to distinguish three types of processes: *urban trade-unionism; urban political movement; and urban ideological movement.* It would be tempting to assume a correlation between these three types and to emphasise the production of urban, political and ideological effects according to whether or not they would be supportive of the dominated classes. But such a coherence between the components of the process and the effects produced does not exist. It is true, however, that there does exist a tendency for purely protest struggles to correlate with positive urban effects, for political struggles to be favourable to the dominated classes, and for ideological struggles to have the effect of reproducing the dominant ideology. But these are only tendencies, for at the same time we are in the presence of effects which are deeply contradictory with this logic.

Now, on its own a protest movement by the dominated classes is not enough to produce positive urban effects; it is also important that the dominant classes have not politicised the stake. This politicisation is largely determined by the content of the stake, and if it takes place the protest movement will not only *not* lead to an urban level, but will also provoke negative effects at the level of the relationship of political forces.

Moreover, the production of ideological effects of contestation is largely due to the political movement and the content of protest which characterises it, this without having to liken ideological movement to ideological reproduction effects. In fact, one of the important aspects of an ideological movement is that protest centred around social relations is not significant at the ideological level, but is on the other hand very important in the creation of a relation of political forces favourable to the dominated classes. Thus so-called 'qualitative' protests are based more on the ability to rally popular support than to change consciousness, and are more directly associated with the experience of political battle.

The one type of process which is closely related with its effect is the political movement; but even in this case the creation of a favourable relation of forces also depends on the involvement of the dominant classes, and on the fact that their involvement may be economic while that of popular mobilisation will be developing towards a political definition. We note once again the defensive character of contemporary popular urban struggles, the control by the dominant classes still determining the process. While this does not irrevocably determine the outcome, it does mean that the practices observed are situated according to such a definition.

The articulation of these effects is extremely important to the general logic of analysis of these movements. Very different processes can lead to the same series of effects, while certain variables, through the interactions between the effects they produce and the reciprocal influence between them, may reinforce or cancel each other.

In short, the analysis of urban struggles must consider social relations in each conjuncture, and, moreover, the emergence of these social movements can only be understood through the study of their articulation to class political relations and to a precise historical situation.

The Place of Urban Movements in the Historical Dynamic of Class Relations in France

While it is certainly true that we cannot take the results of our research as scientific givens, if only because of the frailty of our empirical observations and the difficulty of ascertaining whether these effects are due to the specificity of the conjuncture examined, nevertheless they do open up a new problematic. They can provide some significant bases for reflection, especially since they are congruent to some other more reliable results not presented here. The latter are related to a more elaborate study on protest centred around housing.[4] So far we have demonstrated the need to separate the level of protest from the political level in order to ensure both the success of the protest action and to lead the dominated classes to make changes in the relation of political forces, and this in two ways: for example, the excessive politicisation of the squatting movement led to its isolation, repression and defeat; while the municipal political movement led to an improvement of public facilities and strengthened electoral positions of the Left, but at the same time demobilised and disorganised the popular movement.

We must also mention another significant result which was confirmed by our housing study: the introduction of a political element in a mass movement following successful protest enables politicisation and can lead to political victories proper. In this way we examined the social mechanisms which electoral sociology had previously demonstrated through ecological correlations: the *grands ensembles* contributed to electoral gains for the Left, and this for all social classes. But our study also shows that such a result is not due to a spatial form but to a multi-class mass movement arising from the increasing socialisation of the means of consumption.

Thus directly ideological movements (such as squatting and self-management movements) do not produce significant effects in ideological contestation. They are rather the consequence of positive experiences of political or protest struggles. On the other hand, we have observed the importance of ideologically dominant themes for the mobilisation and political radicalisation of the new petty bourgeoisie (lower management, technicians, etc.). These were important in the co-ownership sectors of the *grands ensembles*.

The observed tendencies on the relationship between protest, politics and ideology in popular urban movements appear to us to be also congruent with a wider historical experience, both in relation to urban struggles themselves and to social movements in general; that is to say, there exists a qualitative leap between popular protest and changes in class relations which cannot develop in a linear way and be entirely autonomous from a basic movement. This classical hypothesis appears to be confirmed by the limitations of the American ghetto movement of the 1960s with its absence of any political perspective, and also by the complete heteronomy *vis-à-vis* other political forces of the Chilean 'movement of *pobladores*'. While this idea may have thrilling Leninist overtones, one tends to insist less on its complement, i.e. the Marxist thesis that the emancipation of the workers can only be through the effort of the workers themselves. This means that a specifically political element can only be grafted on to an *autonomous* popular movement based on the daily experience of the masses.

Our observations also confirm another fundamental idea of the historical experience of the relationship between social movements and ideology. Ideological change is almost never the direct aim of a movement. Moreover, if a movement does have such a goal, it is then utopian – and promptly annihilated by the state apparatus, with the consequence that the effects of such a defeat strengthens the reproduction of the dominant ideology, at times under new forms. Ideological change can occur when the movement is based upon the transformation of the economic and political conditions which determine day-to-day practices. Consciousness can change only by and through the action of an economic and political movement. This said, our research is also related to another less-known classical Marxist thesis (owing to Gramsci): ideological stakes are for certain particular social strata key elements of mobilisation. This means that one must move away from the classical interpretation of development from the economic to the ideological. Very fruitful and efficient struggles can develop, according to the conjuncture and to the classes, through ideological instigation. The point is that they are not *directly* aimed at the transformation of social relations without a political or institutional intermediary. Without these intermediaries struggles are blinded and either become integrated in other projects or crushed by the state apparatus. But the articulation of ideological demands with political or institutional objectives appears to be one of the new and fundamental horizons of certain urban movements currently emerging.

These theoretical analyses which embrace and develop our research findings can perhaps enable us to provide an answer to the *specifically historical question of the emergence of urban social movements in France today*. This question must be understood in terms of the recognition of two facts:

(i) On the one hand it is completely false to say that there are no urban struggles in France. Any investigation in a neighbourhood or suburb will reveal a great number of small, day-to-day struggles involving means of collective consumption. Associations are much richer than one would think, and residents are quite sensitive to problems of the quality of life. In any case, they are as sensitive to these problems as they are to political and economic questions in general.

(ii) But, on the other hand, these great number of struggles and organisations have only a weak social impact and rarely lead to great mass movements. Until recently they have kept a low profile in political struggles and have not developed new social relations – *they are not social movements*.

An explanation to this situation (and the ways it can be overcome) must be found in *the forms of articulation of urban struggle to the historical process of class struggle*. It is only then that our observations and interpretations will acquire full meaning.

Certain analyses in fact attempt to explain the low political and ideological hold of urban struggles in France by stressing the role of state intervention and its power to integrate and disarm potential social movements. To us, such a position is completely ideological and false, both theoretically and historically. For one thing, experience tends to suggest a contrary hypothesis: state policies of integration are more conducive to the development of social movements than are repressive ones. This is illustrated by the American reformist programmes of the 1960s ('War on Poverty' and 'Community Action' in particular) which despite their manipulative intentions made easier popular movements, while Nixon's repressive policies (which so much more clearly could have led to a consciousness about the class nature of the state) put the brake on this movement for a few years.

Besides, the French state appears to be less concerned with integration than other states of comparable societies. On the one hand, it does not operate through special privileges accorded to a particular electoral clientele (as in Christian-democrat Italy) and on the other, because of the relative weakness of the French bourgeoisie, it has rarely initiated social-democratic types of reform for the dominated classes.

As a matter of fact it is in the relationship between urban struggles and class struggles, and in their concentrated expression as class political struggles, that one must seek their different historical roles. For example, it was in this way that the squatting movement in Chile was decisive, for it represented at one and the same time the failure of social-democratic reformism, as well as the incorporation into the popular forces of a critical sector of the proletariat which had been marginal to the major traditionally organised union movements; or, again, urban social movements in the United States which in the 1960s were extremely visible due to their intimate association with ethnic minorities' liberation movements, but which have an entirely different base in the 1970s. This is the common opposition by consumers and producers of public services to the reorganisation of these services as a consequence of the structural economic crisis. Last, urban movements in Italy are currently the most important ones, not because they are the most spontaneous (the opposite is true, as they are largely composed of political militants), or the most culturally innovative (for they are very economistic in their demands), but because they are part of a larger movement which is founded on demands for a complete structural reform and a decisive change in the relation of force between classes.

So, from this viewpoint, what is the situation in France? What has until very recently characterised the French Left and the popular movements it influences has been a juxtaposition between an economic defense of popular living standards, and a political strategy based on the short-term accountability of electoral results. This analysis is also valid for the extreme Left if a daily practice which, without linking them, places side by side defence or denounciation with purely ideological declarations of principle is taken as equivalent. Urban struggles play a double role under these conditions: (i) they can, as they effectively do, defend living conditions at the level of indirect wages; (ii) they can maintain a vague popular dissatisfaction which can, whenever possible, be translated into national or municipal electoral votes. An urban movement cannot as such have a social autonomy, or play a particular political role other than in terms not dissimilar to other anti-monopolist strata such as small shopkeepers.

But now, in Western Europe, and France in particular, this strategic impasse for the Left is being overcome. This overtaking is being done on two fronts: at the level of social democracy (which should not be confused with the Socialist Party), and at the level of a socialist democracy (which should not be confused with the Communist Party – far from it). The first implies a reform of the mechanisms for the redistribution of income which would not affect the economic and ideological hegemony of capital. But, as indirect wages are an essential part of current income, as socialised consumption plays a primary role in the development of social productivity, and as the state can more easily intervene in this sector, 'urban' reforms and urban movements which originate them become an important element in the social-democratic programme. Hence the development in France these last few years of struggles and organisations more or less explicitly related to projects of municipal socialism, which some have purposely confused with self-management.

Furthermore, once the smoke has lifted from the battles of the Winter Palace, the revolutionary project must find new ways to emancipate itself from the alternative between the political ghetto and ideological utopia. Unable to seize the state apparatus, it must then penetrate it, dissolve and transform it. For such an operation not to be one of pure integration in the system, it must be based on the radical transformation of relations of forces outside state institutions, i.e. in civil society, in the practices of the masses and in the last analysis in the heads of the people themselves. But now, if, as we have shown, ideological change arises essentially from a practice in economic and political struggle, protest movements then become the source of ideological and political innovation from which a new society will progressively emerge from the practice of struggle and structural reform. Such a strategy means that the political Left must enlarge its mass support and go beyond its traditional hold in the working-class movement, and this not only because the revolutionary project must count upon a large non-silent majority in order to impose its hegemony on the state apparatus of the dominant classes, but also because the socialisation of labour and the social production of value in advanced capitalism has not only enlarged and diversified the sources of exploitation, but also those of revolt.

Within this new perspective, urban movements are those which most unify the interests of various classes and strata against the dominant structural logic, and which lead them to confront a state apparatus which has become the principal manager of collective goods. Moreover, to the extent that these struggles can bend the dominant structural logic, it can at the same time affect, in certain sectors, the functioning of the state apparatus and trigger its transformation in a more complex and contradictory process. From this viewpoint, urban social movements in France are becoming, whether one wants it or not, the essential sources of the new dynamic of struggle which is implicit in the revolutionary project now developing. We have had some insight of this in the mobilisation of professionals in the *grands ensembles* and in the popular organisations of transport users.

Such a development is not only concerned with the wider political impact of urban movements; it also affects them, for as soon as a protest mass movement produces qualitative effects on class relations (even if this is via political mediation), it becomes more ideologically conscious and politically autonomous and constitutes itself as a social movement. The historical experience of the working-class movement shows that by altering class relations at the political level it has also acquired its autonomy and consciousness at the purely union level. It is by this complex means that the subjective production of social relations and the objectification of the consciousness of this practice become intertwined. More precisely, a popular movement becomes a social movement through the new effects it produces on the politico–ideological relations between classes; and it is by the practical verification of the effects it produces that it becomes conscious of its historical subjectivity and constitutes itself as a social movement on a level different from specifically political relations.

Chapter 7

Ideological Mystification and Social Issues: the Ecological Action Movement in the United States

There were flowers and children's games, young couples in love and hippy communities, and a racial mixture unusual for California. There were trees and animal cries, there was a garden where a few weeks before had stretched a desolate piece of land surrounded by wire netting, an abandoned park destined for use in some vague extension scheme for the University of California at Berkeley. The students decided otherwise; it was to be the 'People's Park'. While troops of volunteers worked on it from day to day, thousands of people relaxed there, enjoying themselves in the spring sunshine; but the university administration deliberated, and Ronald Reagan began shouting about respect for public property. The police received their orders. On 15 May 1969 they occupied the park during the early hours of the morning, destroying the installations and driving out the campers. When the people tried to return to their park, it had become an entrenched camp for 3000 national guards, bayonets fixed. They fired. More than 100 people were shot. Student James Rector never got up again. After a day of manhunts, silence was restored to the park before the arrival of the machines which were to turn it into something for 'public use'.

As for Richard Nixon, the man who poured an unequalled amount of bombs upon the Vietnamese population, in 1969 this man was speaking of the wonderful new prospects open to American civilisation:

I believe that the principal concern in the final third of our century will be the pursuit of happiness. . . . In our future efforts towards universal happiness, there will probably be no more important goal than that of the amelioration of our environment. . . . If we are to materially improve our environment in the months and years to come, the whole of our people must unite in this effort. It will require firm action by the government – at the federal level, at the state level and at the local level. Individual citizens and volunteer groups must unite in this crusade, alongside the world of business and industry, labour and agricultural organisations, education, science and all sectors of society. . . . The unpredictable consequences of our technology have often damaged our environment; henceforth we should appeal to this same technology to restore and preserve it. If I can achieve this, then the next ten years will not merely be the start of our third century as a nation, but also a time of renewal, for the American nation, of unlimited possibilities.[1]

He preaches a return to nature, and then kills those who – admittedly in their own way – follow the good word.

Well, then, do the love of nature and the preservation of the environment constitute a new mystificatory ideology on the part of the American establishment, or a new popular demand charged with revolutionary potential? And if it is a theme which displays both characteristics, how can it be explained? Furthermore, under what conditions and by which processes do ecological movements become the instrument of integration or of conflict?

Two facts which cannot be denied are the power of mobilisation which these problems exercise over a large portion of American youth, and the encouragement this movement receives from political institutions and financial quarters.

Ecological Action: from Conservative Elites to a Protest Movement

Societies for the protection of nature can always be found in the United States, closely linked with the ruling milieu and balancing upon the theme of 'conservation', in the general sense of the term. The most famous of these organisations, the Sierra Club, was founded in 1892 and developed, always at a moderate rate, through its campaign for the creation of national parks to preserve sites of natural beauty. Their members were conservative on the social plane, too, even on their own ground in California: until 1959 the Los Angeles circle refused to admit blacks. The other large association with a membership drawn from the employer class, the Audubon Society, was created in Florida at the start of the century to preserve the wildlife of the Everglades region. As for the great prophet of ecology, Henry David Thoreau, he was nothing but an unimportant Rousseauist for a long time, preaching by some writings and by personal example a return to the wild state which met with little response in a country involved in industrialisation to the death and the establishment of great economic trusts on a world scale.

But these old, tranquil associations, and these themes, forgotten in the rocking chairs of an elite for whom time had stopped, were to be the springboard for a whole torrent of discussions, organisations and actions which first shook the country's large universities and then spread to vast sectors of the population, thus linking, for the first time, student activities and the sleeping Americans of middle-class suburbs. In general the first initiative came from student leaders disappointed by the relative failure of their general protest movement after initial success. The fight for civil rights had revealed the limits of the Black Power theses and led to the decision of militant blacks to count upon their own strength; the campaign against the war in Vietnam had lost its hold since the time when, under pressure from the Vietnamese people, Nixon was about to begin the withdrawal of troops, while continuing to fight a war of a different sort which would touch the American people less directly. The Free Speech Movement and the new demands for organisational democracy were being quietly swallowed up by the liberal universities. Attempts at institutional politicisation (the Macarthy campaign at the 1968 Democratic Convention) had run out of steam when faced by the traditional party machines. In consequence the student movement underwent a serious crisis, whose most striking expression was the split of the only national revolutionary organisation, the S.D.S. (Students for a Democratic Society), at the Chicago Convention in 1969, and the mass migration of a good number of protesters to rural communities where they tried, without success, to set up self-sufficient subcultures.

Thus a student leader from Berkeley, Cliff Humphrey, with no illusions left, formed with his wife and a couple of friends the first Ecology Action Group at this university in 1968. At the same time, some leaders of the World International Party (leftist group) managed to set up a press service on 'ideological emergence', the E.R.O. (Earth Read-out). The process became generalised, always starting from the establishment of a core of converts, who, struck by the evidence of their theses, began to publicise the themes, through film shows, meetings and leaflet distribution. It is interesting to note that the ecological movement arose from programmes pre-established by the militants, whereas the previous mobilisations – minorities, Vietnam, etc. – had expressed themselves more hesitantly and more collectively.

These theses are simple in content and extraordinarily detailed as to examples and concrete support. They often adopt a dramatic, transcendental tone, and call for a return to the source before the fateful day of destruction arrives. It is millenarianism with a nuclear touch, the fearful reflexes of a super-power in difficulties – the ecological theses are all variations upon the following sort of statements:

> The ecological reality of life is frightening. The survival of all living creatures – including man – depends upon the integrity of the complex network of biological phenomena of which earth's ecological system is a part. And yet what man does on earth violates this basic law of human existence. For modern technology affects the ecological system which supports us in a way which threatens its stability; with tragic stubbornness we have linked a large part of our productive economy with aspects of technology which are destructive as far as ecology is concerned. These close, deep connections have enclosed us in a circle of self-destruction. If we want to escape from this suicidal course, we should begin by learning about the ecological realities of life.[2]

These preliminaries of apprenticeship and information were strongly supported by the university institutions, who, in contrast to the previous mobilisation campaigns, opened their doors and offered their resources to the champions of ecology, and organised courses and research on these themes.

As far as concrete measures are concerned, the movement is orientated first and foremost towards the preservation of nature and the 'balance of nature', and in consequence attacks all the sources of pollution of the natural elements – sky, water, sea, calmness of the countryside, food, etc. Cars are condemned (fumes and noise) along with factories (air deterioration), the atom bomb (source of radioactivity) and the war in Vietnam (use of chemical defoliants). People's imaginations are deeply stirred, on the one hand, by the existence of non-perishable waste, notably indestructive plastic materials and car dumps, and on the other by the uncontrolled use of chemical products, e.g. D.D.T., whose harmful effects on the organism appeared to be already proven. On the other hand, urban problems are not considered as such; cities are generally condemned as artificial (not natural) places to live. But even if nature has nothing to do with the city, its problematic is closely linked with that of the population explosion; strict birth control is among one of the most vehement demands of those who seek to defend the balance of nature.

One of the most influential organisations is 'Zero Population Growth', which advocates a total halt to population growth in the United States by 1980, in the rest of the world by 1990. Its president, Ehrlich, wrote the best-seller *The Population Bomb*,[3] which blames over-population for all the evils afflicting our world, and proposes a series of energetic measures to put an end to this, in particular in the 'under-developed' countries – among other things, the addition of sterilising products to the water of large cities, a tax on children, and a luxury tax on baby supplies.

The aim is, in fact, to stop the bringing into the world of an ever-increasing number of men, the principal polluters and destroyers of a nature, upon the preservation of which all life depends.

The social base of such a movement is clearly defined; it is made up of an *avant-garde* of students and youth clubs, and relies on the support of a large portion of the white middle classes who until now have remained outside the social and ideological movements of American society. In this sense the environment movement is connected with the action begun several years ago by Ralph Nader and his American Trial Lawyers Association to defend consumers against the omnipotence of large companies, through dramatic legal actions, of which the most important were those which raised the question of the manufacturer's responsibility for car safety. It is well known that the ideology of Ralph Nader and the consumer associations boils down to an attack on monopolies, while respecting the liberal tenets of free competition and the rules of free individual choice.

Along with the environment theme, this forms a dual return to the past: towards a primitive nature and an economy without monopolies. Nader's style of intervention also influenced the ecological movement; in fact its actions consist essentially of organising public-opinion campaigns which lead to legal proceedings against one decision or another which offends against nature, or else aimed at getting relevant laws enacted. Certainly in the universities there has been a whole series of spectacular actions (burial of car-engines, refuse-bearing processions, anti-pollution marches, etc.), but they are above all publicity stunts intended to get pressure to be put on the institutions. A key point is that in all these battles it is a question of a claim whose justification is recognised by the leaders of society and the mass media at a general ideological level. On the other hand, there is hardly any response within minority groups: blacks, Puerto Ricans, Chicanos and Indians have remained outside the movement except for a purely tactical utilisation of it to support specific claims made in connection with other objectives.

Perhaps this has something to do with the increasing political radicalisation of these minorities, whereas one of the basic characteristics of the ecological movement is the way it ignores ideological frontiers. Observers in the American press have complacently remarked upon this; members of the John Birch Society and S.D.S. leftists are found side by side. It is said that in the face of the biological problem of survival all people have merged into one Boy Scout army, ready to defend nature against technology regardless of class and political regime. Unfortunately for these visionaries, a cursory examination shows that the mobilised social base belongs, in a large majority, to the white middle-class layers of society, to the ruling elite, to the liberal professions and high-ranking white-collar workers. The important new element, by comparison with the traditionally middle-class movements, is the joining, within the ecological movement, of these layers with the radicalised student faction in recent years. It is this situation which must be analysed and explained, especially since the paradox is pushed to an extreme by the thematic and organisational coincidence between this new 'protest' movement and the new problematic of the American ruling elite.

The Great Manoeuvres of the 'Eco-establishment'

The Nixon administration's insistence upon the protection of the environment while hushing up the half-hearted reforms attempted beforehand is well known; the war on poverty, the Model Cities Programme and the timid efforts at racial integration were replaced (they were said to be out of date) by a policy presenting itself as forward-looking and concerned with the very foundations of human happiness. In the official speeches and the few measures which have been taken, with a copious supply of bureaucratic machinery, these *leitmotifs* seemed to suggest more or less the end of History; after conquering Nature by Technology, after brushing with the catastrophe of the destruction of the first by the second, we were returning to a comfortable

Nature with the assistance of a technology freed from its un-controllable appetite, and tamed within an ecological balance which was to bring social balance. In a word, communism was opposed by a return to the primitive community, within a system based on free enterprise.

The largest American firms fell into line, creating research centres, preparing the mass production of 'natural products' and anti-pollution systems, launching vast publicity campaigns and support-ing this movement of public opinion which had finally turned away from the old arguments about social inequality.

The great reconciliation between state, monopolies and protesting students was Earth Day on 22 April 1970. On that day millions of people, with students in the forefront, took part in great public dem-onstrations all over the country, to preach the protection of nature through civism and a return to a simple life style. Meetings, marches and 'good deeds' took place one after the other.[4]

It was something of a combination of peace rallies and the Wood-stock crowds, but there was also the astonishing unanimity of the American nation, which had suddenly rediscovered its community feeling, endangered in recent times by a new, protesting youth. But this time they were only too willing to satisfy this youth; all over the country important public personalities addressed meetings; the pre-paratory text for the day, *The Environmental Handbook* received quasi-official approval from the White House, and above all *the large trusts financed the organisation of the day* (among them, for example, Proctor and Gamble, General Electric, Goodrich, Du Pont, Standard Oil of New Jersey, International Paper, Philips Petroleum, Coca-Cola, Chevron Oil, General Motors, Atlantic Richfield). 'Big business re-sponsibility'? Possibly, but when you consider the position and the action of the trusts as regards other protest movements, there is cause for surprise and for questioning the underlying interests of such a unanimity, where alongside 'all the children of the world', a good number of 'big bad wolves' join hands also.

Criticism by the Left: Ideology of Environment and New Forms of Capitalist Profit

It is this which explains the vigour of the criticisms directed at the environment problematic by the American Left, both from the ideological point of view and from that of the underlying economic interest.

In fact, if you think about the implicit content of the themes centred around the environment issue, it becomes apparent that this ideology makes social conflict something natural, by reducing history to a relationship between Man and Nature, a combination of pre-existing resources. We are therefore refering to a metaphysical essence, a 'previous state' which has been lost, damaged, soiled by the subordination to technological imperatives which are indispensable since it is by technical progress that living standards are raised. The concrete effect of this ideology is striking; all the flaws in what we call 'daily life', i.e. the collective conditions of consumption and social relationships, are gathered together under one label which presents them as a natural calamity (*naturally technological*) against which the only possible defence is to mobilise all 'men of goodwill' without exception, enlightened and supported by their government. The ideology of environment, 'apolitical', humanitarian, universalist and scientific, transforms social inequality into mere physical inconveniences and blends the social classes into one army of Boy Scouts. And yet the direct link between the search for private profit and the neglect of 'social costs' when calculating profitability, which has become the first norm of social functioning, is well known.

Furthermore, the Left-wing militants shed light not only on the responsibility of capitalist mechanisms in the production of pollution[5] but also on the existence of a whole industrial complex for manufacturing and installing pollution-control systems, made up essentially of those large firms whose activity is at the source of the worst pollution![6] This branch of activity is expecting an annual growth rate of 20 per cent in the next few years, i.e. three times that of heavy industry. And this new market is steadily being taken over by the industrial groups classed as major sources of pollution: Dow Chemical, Monsanto Chemical, W. R. Grace, Du Pont, Merck, Nalco, Union Carbide, General Electric, Westinghouse, Combination Engineering, Honeywell, Beckman Instruments, Alcoa, Universal Oil Products, North American Rockwell, etc. Thus, while not denying the deterioration of the conditions of everyday life, the Left posed the question of what mechanisms lie behind this crisis, at the same time refusing to see in this the major issue in American society.

To these theoretical criticisms of the ideology of environment and the underlying interests must be added the practical criticism which the most active groups among the American national minorities expressed, *by not expressing themselves*: Black Panthers, Puerto Ricans of the Young Lords Party, Chicanos and Indians, all seem to scorn these themes, and insist rather upon the living conditions in their ghettos, less in terms of environment than in terms of discrimination and oppression as they have been doing for several years.[7] They fight for decent housing, for playgrounds for the children, but not for the safeguard of nature; they fight against the property speculators, against town councils in the service of the middle classes, against police bullying, which, for example, prevents them from turning on the fire hydrants in the street to combat the heat of summer in an American town.

This indifference to the environment crusade on the part of those who still constitute, despite the crises, the spearhead of the American Left cannot but reinforce one's scepticism as to the prospects of social innovation offered by the ecological movement; it confirms the criticisms of this nature ideology, and offers a warning against the risks of manipulation to which student youth, lacking political maturity, is subject.

And yet the reality and the range of a social problem must not be confused with the social treatment which it receives. In other words, even if it is true that the deterioration of our communal heritage is expressed in the terms of the dominant ideology, and the trusts even try to profit from it (as from everything, since anything can be turned to good use by capitalism), we are also dealing with a reality experienced by people which obviously has social causes, not 'technical' or 'biological' ones. As soon as this state of affairs is revealed, entire pieces of the capitalist logic are in danger of collapsing. Just imagine, for example, the consequences a real boycott of cars would have on an automobile industry which lies at the heart of the trust system! It is true that electric engines could be a way out, but the depreciation in value of all that exists already and the all-powerful interests of the petrol trusts have to be taken into account. It has been proved that this is the principal source of pollution, but who would dare to question the activity of these giants, their goodwill in introducing new technical procedures and their opportunities of drilling and working oil wells? There is therefore 'good' and 'bad' protest about the environment, and the neglect of these problems by private enterprises has – in certain cases and *for certain social levels* – enabled a first shadow of doubt to be cast over the truth of the famous slogan 'What is good for General Motors is good for the United States. Perhaps this explains why in official circles there is a tendency to refuse responsibility for pollution and place it on the urban phenomenon, i.e. ultimately on each citizen, polluting with every gesture he makes, so that consequently the only action that can be taken is through civism and self-discipline, by good ecological, biological and, of course, social behaviour.

This also explains another highly significant but little-known fact: although the protection of the environment has become a *leitmotif* of many official speeches, *the concrete measures taken by government policy are in a state of stagnation, and the progress made in the fight against pollution is virtually nil*; Between 1965 and 1970, the portion of the federal budget devoted to environmental programmes was steadily *decreasing* (see Table 12).

TABLE 12   *Portion of Federal Budget devoted to environment*

Year	Percentage of budget
1965	2.3%
1966	2.2%
1967	2.0%
1968	1.9%
1969	1.9%
1970	1.8%

SOURCE: Barry Weisburg, 'The Politics of Ecology', *Liberation Magazine* (January 1970).

On the other hand, the main anti-pollution measures which could have been taken either were not taken at all, or were taken in an inefficient way. For example, there has been no definition of the pollution levels of differently composed fuels, which makes any control entirely subjective, nor is any control exercised over the drilling of oil wells – Congress refused to abolish the 1872 mining law which allows any individual to carry out excavations or digging in search of oil, with no limits other than property rights; no general system of stream cleansing was envisaged, so as not to get in the way of the functioning of the local systems (very inefficient) which represent all sorts of economic and political interests in each town. This procrastination is not surprising if one is acquainted with the business connections of the top personnel in the eco-establishment: Bert S. Cross, appointed president of the National Industrial Pollution Control Board by Nixon, is also president of the Minnesota Mining and Manufacturing company, which has been condemned for polluting the Mississippi with sulphurous products; John Blatnik, president of the Congress sub-committee on pools and rivers, represents the interests of taconite mining, one of the chief sources of pollution on Lake Superior; even Democrat Senator Muskie, presidential candidate and fervent activist for the environment, is limited in his enthusiasm by his position as defender of the oil industry's interests – he is planning to set up a highly pollutive complex right in the middle of his state, Maine, one of the priority natural zones for preservation!

Thus the theme of environment appears to be one massive misunderstanding, where issues and attempts at manipulation become entangled in a rigorous dialectic between integration and questioning. So one is obliged to reject the generalisation of the ecological movement considered as a unity and to attempt to differentiate the types of intervention in terms of the structural composition of the objectives involved and the social base effectively mobilised.

Typology of Movement for Environmental Defence: Some Examples

If we are to understand, rather than judge, a form of social mobilisation so complex and so original as the American ecological movement, we must distinguish a whole series of situations, ranging from participation to protest, according to the social group and the issue involved.

First, there are many cases of mobilisation where middle-class elites took the initiative on a theme which involved little risk for the dominant social interests, and for which it was easy to win popularity. This was the case with one of the environment defenders' most successful actions: the preservation of San Francisco Bay, whose coastal public property was being gradually invaded by buildings. Realising that this was a simple case of property speculation, profiting property groups to the detriment of the natural heritage of· the Californian coast, a committee was formed, composed mostly of teachers and high-ranking white-collar workers. It sought the support of public opinion and put pressure on the provincial chamber in the best lobbying tradition of American pressure groups. By means of a good press campaign and massive public support (2,000,000 signatures), the committee obtained, in 1969, the voting through of a law requiring the granting of a building permit for any new undertaking which would affect the bay. It is interesting to note that the government proposed the introduction of a special tax for bay-side dwellers to subsidise this system: almost total victory, an action perfectly respectful of institutions, objectives shared by all the groups, no very powerful interests (only some property groups) – such an action is a perfect illustration of the 'practical politics for good citizens' underlying the environment ideology.

On the other hand, mobilisation on the same social level, the middle classes led by high-ranking professions, takes on quite a different significance when the issue brings important interests into play. Such was the case with the vigorous campaign led by a group of Cornell University scientists, with the support of a part of the population, against the installation of a nuclear-power station near Lake Cayuga in the north of New York State. After founding a lake-side residents' committee and presenting a scientific report setting out the dangers the population would be subjected to, the defenders of the natural peace of this zone managed to halt this project (emanating from a private company) towards the end of 1969.[8] The interests which were put in the balance by this were considerable: a generalisation of this protest could affect the vigorous future policies of large American firms. This type of action, first as legalist as in the San Francisco Bay affair, is possibly moderate, but the objective results of the process are not. Thus the theme of environment turns against its prophets.

Furthermore, when ecological action develops in a student milieu which is not yet ready to forget its revolutionary inclinations, highly explosive connections can be created between a socially legitimate claim and analyses which are somewhat less conservative than those of campers' clubs. Thus side by side with the naturalist rambles of the Sierra Club there is anti-capitalist mobilisation on the part of other student groups, supported in their principles if not in their methods by a large proportion of public opinion. Thus in 1970 after the pollution of the beaches at Santa Barbara in California by the activities of Union Oil, the students stormed and burned the headquarters of the Bank of America, the real master of Union Oil, claiming at the same time that this bank was taking an active part in policies of racial discrimination, youth-hunting, and the Vietnam war. This demonstrated how the connection between these issues and the theme of environment, better understood by the non-mobilised majority of the population, can become explosive in the literal sense of the word.

This is also what happens in the case of mobilisation in black ghettos centred around specifically urban objectives. The 1967 riots often had as their *pretext* (and not as their cause, as is sometimes claimed) the lack of community facilities, especially of green spaces and playgrounds in the poor quarters,[9] and the fight against the demolition of those ghettos included in the urban redevelopment plans was at the root of several mass confrontations with the police and the town planners. Here it was a matter of defending the ghetto as the ecological base of a social and political community which was affirming its autonomy with thoughts of its liberation in mind. The fight for environment thus signifies in such cases – by reinforcing it – a class struggle.[10]

Having said this, the reason for such a diversity of situations and processes within the ecological movement is the ever-changing combination of a certain number of basic elements whose predominance or subordination explains the social content of each action.

The Internal Components of the Ecology Movement, or 'Why Everyone Seems to Agree'

The variety of politico–ideological registers within the mobilisation over environment arises from the contradictory diversity of its social costs.

It seems correct to link the new anti-pollution industry and urban land-use to the process called by economists *devaluation of social capital* which constitutes one of the basic characteristics of present-day capitalism. It is a question of halting the tendency towards decreased profits by the state taking on an increasing number of non-profitable investments, thus creating new openings and at the same time enabling profits to stay high in the sectors which have remained private. Public intervention in the realm of the environment seems generally to have immense possibilities for development, a fact which allows the massive use of financial resources (without drawing on public funds, i.e. the taxpayers) to be justified.

But the economy is not the only thing. The theme of environment takes up, extends and renews the classic model of local participation upon which American political life was built. How can the impetus of this community action, the very basis of liberalism, be maintained at a time when urban growth and cities are overrunning the limits of daily living space, and when local authorities have hardly any power of decision any longer over the essential problems of daily life? The environment crusade gives rise to a sort of super-community taking in the nation as a whole, without losing the stamp of the 'family' style of political intervention and of the middle classes' political model, with a great shared theme and different interpretations which confront each other politely by means of lobbying institutions which are not questioned.

This traditional model, despite being combined with it in the same environment theme, is opposed to the new youth counter-culture, which is naturalistic, anti-consumption, refuses to chase after mythical success and attacks the very roots of the productivist values of profitability. In this sense the ecology movement and the idea of a return to nature and rejection of industrialisation and science represent a real *revolutionary utopia*, complete with all the issues presented by the linking of these two terms in this way. The rejection of 'post-industrial society' is at one and the same time a symptom of revolt and an acceptance of the ideology according to which the age of abundance has arrived, and all that remains for us to do is to gather in the (natural) fruits of the long march of humanity. This is the *idealistic Left-wing* aspect of the environment theme, which is the way the theme is formulated within the student movement.

There is another element in this complex and fluctuating combination; it concerns the collective-consumption conditions of large sectors of the population, especially in the large cities doomed to obsolescence. Here the appeal to nature is a cry of protest, an ideological escape, but also a rejection, laden with political significance, of the conditions of daily life offered by the richest country in the world. What characterises the ecology movement is precisely the fusion of these elements in a paradigm which ignores social differences and puts conflicts down to the opposition between Technology and Nature.

As a paradigm, then, the environment theme is a real ideological mystification, of which we have already shown the underlying interests. But as a social practice linked with trends as charged with significance as these we have just described, the ecology movement expresses the real social issues daily experienced by the masses. But the link with political practice – which alone can bring about change – cannot come about unless the revolutionary elements, today in a subordinate position within the ecology movement (the utopian counter-culture and the claims over collective consumption), become the very pivot of the movement.

Thus the fight for the environment in the United States will either remain a vast mystification undertaking, or become a powerful lever of change. It all depends on the ability of the political movements to recognise and direct these new urban social movements.

Chapter 8

City, Class and Power

Urban problems are increasingly at the heart of political debate in industrial capitalist societies. The Italian Left obtained a majority in the 1975 municipal elections in all the large towns, in part on the basis of urban protests and partly on the strength of being an alternative form of local government. The same phenomenon occurred in Japan, where socialists and communists, because they have given priority to urban and environmental issues, govern the most important cities. In the United States, the crisis of New York is only the most spectacular manifestation of a series of social contradictions which question a model of urban development which nevertheless remains indispensable for the organisation of an existence centred around the dominant interests of American society. In France, urban and regional policies are one of the clearest indicators of the cleavages and struggles between different political forces, as could be observed during the debate on the Galley Bill (which in 1975 tried to tax more heavily speculative use of land and triggered widespread opposition from the business circles), or yet still, in the successive measures which have been adopted with respect to public transport and urban-renewal programmes. The middle classes are living increasingly in the *grands ensembles*, and some observers have gone as far as to attribute the success of the Left in the 1976 district elections to their dissatisfaction with the lifestyle in these new residential milieux. As we shall see, this process is in fact more complex.

If in addition to institutional expressions of political power we observe the evolution of popular movements, one of the most significant phenomena of recent years has been the birth of social protests and demands concerned with urban and environmental questions. Through these different ways, the city and its problems appear to have increasing importance in the practice of power. This relationship also develops in an opposite way, in that political power, the state being its concentrated expression, increasingly shapes the city. State intervention in the city, both direct and indirect, is a fundamental element in the organisation of the public resources which constitute the urban structure.[1]

Where does this urban politicisation come from? And where is it leading to? At one level it is the result of a contradictory process engendered by the economic and social evolution of advanced capitalism. The concentration of capital leads to concentration of the means of production and units of management, as well as concentration of the necessary labour force. The spatial concentration of workers determines the concentration of the means of consumption which they need. This relates as much to private individual consumption (goods sold on the market) as to collective consumption (indivisible goods and services). Moreover, the increasing interdependence of the various units of production and management compels the smooth functioning of the whole economic complex, in production as well as in consumption.

The State and Collective Consumption

These processes are at the basis of the urban structure of large cities. Now, with technological development, the labour force enlarges its role in the process of production: each worker must make productive the increasingly larger portions of capital invested in machines; the interdependence of technical and economic units requires the increasingly programmed functioning of the labour force; finally, the acceleration of technological progress reinforces the role of information and knowledge, and as a consequence, requires increasing skills in the creation of value from *one section* of the labour force. The strategic role of the labour force correspondingly increases the role of the means of collective consumption necessary to it, especially public resources and facilities. Housing, schools, crèches and nurseries, health services, cultural activities, transport, and so on, all have become essential to the urban structure and to the requirements of the production process. Could one possibly imagine a labour market without a transport system capable of distributing mostly at the same time each day workers all over the city?

These means of collective consumption also play a fundamental role in the organisation of private commodity consumption. For example, the growth of the car industry depends entirely upon the organisation of an inter-city rapid transit network. The implantation of large suburban shopping centres, at the basis of a renewal of a certain kind of consumption, itself depends on housing and transport policies, as well as on the state of the property market. Now, one knows that one of the most essential problems of advanced capitalism is that of finding new markets able to keep up with the mass of capital which must be made productive and profitable.

The stimulation of demand, which becomes fundamental for private capital, goes through a series of mechanisms (credits, fiscal policies, publicity, etc.), one of which is the mode of organisation itself and consumption arising from the provision of public facilities. For example, American residential suburbs (and also probably French ones, though at this stage we can assert it only for the United States) are powerful instruments for the stimulation of commodity consumption. But these suburbs, and this model of implicit behaviour and consumption, have been made possible by a certain kind of urban policy of which the state has been a major instrument.[2]

Thus, if it is true that our society remains first and foremost determined by the process of production, collective consumption, while remaining a secondary contradiction, is acquiring an increasingly important role in social organisation. This said, public resources are required not only by production and consumption processes, but they also respond to the development of popular demands, whose needs are defined historically, simultaneously and proportionately, by the progress of the productive forces, and especially by the reversal of relations of force between classes in struggle. As the working-class movement acquired strength and political influence in advanced capitalist countries, the direct wage received from employers has increasingly been supplemented by an indirect wage, socially levied, and by collective goods and services which often become more important for the popular living standard than the nominal amount of direct wages.[3]

It is in this way, as capitalism develops, that the means of collective consumption at the basis of the urban structure are required increasingly by the evolution of capital, production and consumption processes, and social demands. Now, at the same time it so happens that, usually, the production and management of most of these collective goods are not profitable for private capital – at least not unless an intervention external to capital has established the prior conditions necessary to capitalist profit. The reasons for this are too complex to summarise in one sentence, but one could say that they are related to the historical relations between classes, not to the 'nature' of these goods and services themselves.[4]

This leads us on to a major contradiction of capitalist development: the logic of capital cannot fulfill a diversity of fundamental demands. It is in an attempt to resolve this contradiction that the state decisively intervenes in the production, distribution and management of the means of collective consumption and spatial organisation of these services.[5] Collective equipment and the resulting urban system will therefore be decisively affected by the role of the state. In France, if one takes state expenditure by budgetary item as an approximate indicator of the evolution of state intervention, and if this is expressed in terms of percentage of national revenue, one can observe a sharp reversal of expenditure according to function. The traditional political functions of defense and administration have risen from 5 per cent of G.N.P. in 1870 to 9.9 per cent in 1970; state assistance to agriculture, industry and commerce have risen from 0 per cent to 2.9 per cent; and expenditures which can be classified as 'collective goods and services' (education, culture, social programmes, transport, housing and urbanisation) have risen from 1 to 14.1 per cent over this period.[6]

However, this intervention is not a simple regulating mechanism. The action of the state is the result of a political process which is largely determined by class struggle. Political conflicts will therefore be determinant in the management of the means of collective consumption and the urban system. Now, to the extent that these condition social practices, social groups are affected by state intervention in this domain, the state becoming the *actual manager of collective services structuring daily life*. Contradictions developing in the sphere of collective consumption, and conflicts originating in urban organisation, tend therefore to be more or less directly reflected back on to state intervention and underlying political trends. State intervention in the city, while attempting to overcome the contradictions resulting from the inability of producing the goods and services it urgently needs, in fact *politicises* and *globalises* urban conflicts by articulating directly the material conditions of daily life and the class content of state policies.

The Working Class, the New Petty Bourgeoisie and the Democratic Road to Socialism

Such an evolution is fundamental from a political viewpoint, because what characterises urban contradictions is that they concern all popular classes, including the 'new petty bourgeoisie' (technicians and clerks). The housing crisis extends itself far beyond the working class; the crisis in public transport concerns everyone who must make a daily journey to work; the lack of crèches and nurseries affects all women; the social and functional segregation of space is beneficial only to the minute minority making up the power elite; pollution is itself also largely indivisible; and so on. But if these contradictions affect a large majority of the population, they are not necessarily 'natural' or specific to an 'urban milieu'; they are determined by historically defined social relations. , In our societies they originate *in their specific form* from the capitalist organisation of production and consumption, and from state intervention which is largely dominated by the power bloc constituted around the hegemonic fraction of finance capital.

It is therefore through urban contradictions that the dominant social logic affects the popular classes in a largely indivisible way. Residents and commuters react by means of various protest movements which are virtually becoming a form of *urban trade unionism*.[8] One must take special notice of the particularly significant participation in these movements of the new petty bourgeoisie,[9] which in employment has had a relatively weak tradition of struggle and organisation. *Urban struggles* have been the means whereby popular strata traditionally distant from the organisation and orientation of the working-class movement (in part due to their place in the social division of labour) have become conscious of their objective opposition to state practices marked by the hegemony of monopoly capital.[10] The formation of units of collective consumption (large cities) therefore leads to the collective organisation of protest by all classes with regards to these provisions, state intervention often inciting the politicisation of protest.

The implication of this *tendency* can be better understood if they are related to the recent evolution of political expression of popular social movements. For the past twenty-five years, while biding its time and defending the interests of its workers, the Left of Western Europe has been divided between the social-democratic management of capitalism and political isolation. The social struggles which have taken place since 1968, the economic crisis, the political weakening of the bourgeoisie in power, have given rise to a new situation. In Italy, in France, but also by other means in other countries, a new political alternative, which some have called the *democratic road to socialism*, is taking shape. It attempts to go beyond the nostalgia of the Winter Palace without nevertheless naively accepting the neutrality of the state from the viewpoint of its class content. The purpose is to go forward by controlling state institutions through democratic means (essentially electoral ones) and transforming social relations, without which economic measures can only lead to a rationalisation of the existing system. How can a class analysis of the state be reconciled to such a strategy? By employing a 'new arm' which should be decisive in the historical phase we are living: the ability to win popular adherence, to gain its conscious support even before controlling these institutions. And the only method known for changing consciousness through the defence of objective interests is the discovery of these interests *in and by struggle*. To be certain, in order to move away from a 'street-fighting' imagery of social struggles, an essential condition is to integrate all the means available for exercising pressure, including the management of sectors or levels of the state.

If the working class is that class which is the most conscious of its situation, and which most supports political organisations which are alternatives to the power organised around the bourgeoisie, it is mostly because it has an experience of organisation and struggle, even though these are derived from its fundamental place in the production process. Now, the working class cannot on its own, in the 1970s, pose a socialist alternative in Western Europe. This can be possible only by the organisation of popular classes *objectively interested* in going beyond capitalism and *subjectively conscious* of this necessity and possibility. While the working class remains a fundamental axis of the socialist project, the social strata essential in broadening the basis for its realisation are the salaried classes which are known as the new petty bourgeoisie. And if these are now struggling in their work-places, it is in urban protest that they most easily discover a similarity of interests with the working class, and a common opposition to the logic of the system and its concentrated expression in the state management of collective resources.

It is in this sense that urban struggles, municipal political alternatives, the debate around collective consumption and city planning, play a crucial role in the present political dynamic. If the *grands ensembles* are voting Left, it is not because of the alienation of concrete housing but because the socialisation of consumption expressed thereof brings together the residents, reinforces their solidarity and promotes the development of struggles which are addressed both to the state as economic agent and to its local and national political apparatus.

This tendency, which is becoming increasingly apparent, is all the more paradoxical in that it is the dominant classes which initially posed 'the urban question' at the forefront of the political scene, in an attempt to substitute the contradiction between labour and capital with problems of the quality of life.[11] This implicit attempt to 'naturalise' social contradictions, and thus to define their solution as a technical problem, has stumbled upon a major 'oversight': the quality of life is not a context, but a practice, and if it is practice which leads to the discovery that there were indeed new social contradictions in the organisation of cities, these moreover are closely articulated to the *ensemble* of class relations, i.e. to relations of power. This is why the relation between the city and power appears to us to be at the centre of the current urban problematic, for, if it is power which structures the city, the movements which it gives birth play a strategic role in the transformation of power.

Chapter 9

Conclusion: the New Frontiers of Urban Research

The analyses presented here have given us the opportunity to appraise a gradual transformation of what has been understood as 'urban' in advanced capitalist countries, both in practice as well as in theory. The most distinctive feature is that *urban politics* are at the centre of the urbanisation process, and that they play an increasingly important part in the whole of the political process as such. It therefore becomes essential to understand the relations between power and the city in order to grasp the meaning of one and the other. Furthermore, these relations become intelligible only when they are introduced within the general dynamic of social classes. This dynamic does not simply refer to the social inequality between socio-professional groups, but is first and foremost defined by the historical process of the class struggle; that is to say, relations between power and the city must be studied from the viewpoint of the ability each class develops in orientating social organisations according to its interests, among which are its intervention in the sphere of the social practices of the city.

We have been able to outline the way this sphere generally corresponds in *advanced capitalism* to the production, distribution and management of the means of collective consumption. A first result from the new urban research was to break away from the ideological carcan of the urban, and to have shown the structural origins of this problematic in the changes undergone by monopoly capitalism. The contradictions it developed in the sector of collective goods and services lead to an intervention by the state which, far from regulating the process, exacerbated contradictions and politicised the issue. This is what we can deduce from our analyses of the urban-renewal programme in Paris, or of urban planning in Dunkirk. Urban politics are therefore at the basis of the urban structure, but it is from the action of the state which the whole of society expresses its orientations and its relations of force. Our study of the evolution of urban policy in France shows to what extent it is linked to the transformation of social classes, to the confrontation of their interests, and to the expression of their political strategies. In addition, we have been able to appreciate to what extent urban policies have been part of a much wider political struggle, and, as such, their impact cannot be reduced simply to social groups which have designs on the city. Sometimes it is through city politics that substantial changes are produced in the power relationships between classes.

Perhaps what is newest in the successive contributions of our research is that the mode of determination of the society upon the urban is not unilateral; it is not a reproduction of capital, but an expression of contradictions between classes. The dominated classes oppose the strategies and interests of the dominant classes and put forward their own alternatives, and this, at one and the same time, both inside and outside the action of the state: on the one hand, through mass movements which are increasingly constituting a second front of social conflict, along with the trade-union movement – we have attempted to trace the conditions of the emergence of these urban social movements, as well as their ambiguities; on the other hand, through the action of the state itself, which throughout the history of domination of the dominant classes has been decisively constituted by it, but which is also the expression of the dominated classes within the limits of the relation of forces they have been able to establish. However, this would entail a much more thorough study of democratic urban and municipal policies than we have so far achieved.

The acquired knowledge of the practical and theoretical fields of the urban must now be more fully developed. In this double movement, it is the development of new historical practices which becomes decisive. How is this question posed at present? What makes it new, and what are the perspectives of its practices in advanced capitalism?

In the first place, the *urban fiscal crisis*, which has for a number of years been affecting most large cities, demonstrates the structural limits, within the framework of dominant capitalist relations, of the increasing socialisation of public services. State intervention in the maintenance of essential but unprofitable public services has effectively been carried out at the cost of an inflationary and growing public debt, for the financing of these growing and indispensable public expenses could not be achieved through an imposition on capital (which refused to yield part of its profits), or, completely, through increased taxation – the eventual social struggles and political oppositions spelled out the limits of such a strengthening of state power at the expense of wage-earners. But from the moment the economic crisis threatened the stability of the circulation of capital because of uncontrollable inflation, one could witness a sudden halt in public expenditure, particularly in the area of public services. This was exercised through two principal mechanisms:

(1) Increasing state control on communes and regions, raising the level of local rates, and considerably reducing public-services budgets.

(2) The refusal by public and private financial institutions to issue loans to local and regional institutions. It is within this perspective that one should examine the fiscal crisis of New York and other large American cities, the increase in local rates in the United Kingdom, the drastic reduction of municipal budgets imposed by the Italian government upon all large cities administered by the Left, the blocking of most social programmes in the Paris region, and so on. The first line of attack of the economic crisis has been that of a policy of austerity imposed by the dominant capitalist groups, and which has taken the form of a questioning of the socialised functions of production, exchange and consumption which were to have been undertaken by the local governments of large cities. The urban fiscal crisis is, in reality, the crisis of the Welfare State, and appears as the most immediate expression of a fundamental transformation of the historical model of capitalist accumulation which had prevailed since the Second World War.

This phenomenon is linked to the appearance and development of the *ecological question*, which is increasingly situated at the centre of the debate on the characteristics and objectives of the mode of economic and social organisation. In fact, the criticism of the ecologists, who are becoming increasingly influential, go beyond the problems of the preservation of nature. Despite their political ambiguity and their intellectual confusions, even at times their naïve naturalism, they denounce the growing contradiction between the characteristics of a model of accumulation and their resulting consequences at the level of social organisation. The more society emphasises, at the cultural level, use value over exchange value (that is, the more everyday happiness becomes more important than the acquisition of commodities) the more absurd it becomes to accumulate for accumulation's sake. But capital cannot stop itself, it must continue to invest, to produce surplus value and to realise it as commodities, even if it means crushing its own productive agents, and even if this includes the executive level. Metropolitan hugeness, the destruction of natural resources, the decline in living standards, the massification of mores and the individualistic savagery of practices thus appear as the side of the coin whose other side is minted in the hallucinating design of an uncontrollable world monopoly capitalism. Therefore, while the questions which the ecologists pose may seem naïve, they fundamentally question the social relations of exploitation and domination. It is a search for open spaces instead of shopping centres, solar energy instead of nuclear plants, social facilities instead of commercial ones, community interaction instead of the mass media, local autonomy instead of a technocratic pseudo-planning. These are not just the themes of professional symposia. They constitute a questioning of the material organisation of daily life by capital and by the state.

In this way the development of the ecological critique appears as an essential historical reference point which demands the formulation of new thinking on the organisation of relations between society and cities, between the mode of economic growth and the forms of social life.

Now, if these and other questions at the basis of urban policy are being strongly posed in the 1970s, it is because *new urban social movements* have given rise to them. At an initial level, the protest movements have extended to the sphere of social consumption the permanent battle engaged upon by the labour movement at the level of mass living standards. The housing crisis gave rise to tenants' organisations. Refusing to accept the transport crisis, commuters' associations put forward new proposals for transport in the large cities. Rejecting the lack of facilities and the centralisation of their management, neighbourhood associations have made their interests felt in urban development. But this questioning of urban organisation is not simply that of the defense of resident interests, it also relates to the opposition to relations of domination. For example, the feminist movement is threatening the very logic of the urban structure, for it is the subordinate role of women which enables the minimal 'maintenance' of its housing, transport and public facilities. In the end, if the system still 'works' it is because women guarantee unpaid transportation (movement of people and merchandise), because they repair their homes, because they make meals when there are no canteens, because they spend more time shopping around, because they look after others' children when there are no nurseries, and because they offer 'free entertainment' to the producers where there is a social vacuum and an absence of cultural creativity. If these women who 'do nothing' ever stopped to do 'only that', the whole urban structure as we know it would become completely incapable of maintaining its functions. The contemporary city also rests upon the subordination of 'women consumers' to the 'men producers'. The subversive nature of the feminist movement is not due to its demand for more nurseries, but to the refusal henceforth onwards to look after anything at all!

In the same way the rise of a labour movement which through its diverse ideological tendencies poses the question of the organisation of the whole of the workers' existences, linking work and residence, 'work' time with 'free' time, living standards with quality of life, proposing new principles for urban services. For example, the 150 hours of general training at the expense of the employer, won by the Italian unions, have shattered the relationship between the university and the world of work, in the same way that in France the democratic urbanism of the Left municipalities has shortened travelling time and improved the industrial working conditions of many workers.

Finally, the growing demand for self-management or for a democratic control of public services has tended to alter profoundly the relationship not only between the state and its citizens but also between citizens and the organisations which represent them. The strengthening of this movement leads to a growing political stake which in our societies is represented by the management of *local and regional governments*. One knows that in Italy (in 1975) and in France (in 1977), the takeover of the municipalities of many large cities by the forces of the Left has been a determining factor for the transformation of relations of power between classes, for the concrete affirmation of a superior ability at social and institutional organisation beginning from a popular and democratic orientation. The overwhelming victory of the Left in the large cities of Italy in June 1975 has enabled the eradication of corruption in local administration, the development of social services (within the limits imposed by the central state), the rationalisation of management, as well as its decentralisation, with the establishment of directly elected neighbourhood councils. But also in the United States there has been in recent years a powerful reformist and populist movement, which on the basis of the liberal

and radical issues of the 1960s have chosen local and state administrations as privileged means of posing alternatives to public policy. It
has already conquered many cities, including state capitals Austin
(Texas) and Madison (Wisconsin) and strongly influences certain
black mayors of large cities. Certainly, this leftward movement is not
progressing in a linear fashion. There is a two-way movement in every
political battle. In 1977, the large English cities were taken over by the
Conservatives; but, in reality, this is a confirmation of the tendency
mentioned previously: local governments have become essential for
the management of the daily lives of the popular masses. They will
therefore express their political choices according to the platforms
and the *practices* of the forces present. Municipal and regional politics,
as institutional expression of urban policy, is becoming one of the
major axes of the political confrontation of classes in advanced capitalism.

It is from the questions posed by these new social and political practices that one must reconsider the urban problematic. To answer
them new researches must be developed, new theories elaborated
which could relate to the current historical process. The new urban
research must consider urgently a number of themes which appear as
central theoretical issues. They refer to current changes in the process
of consumption, to the elaboration of a theory of social movements,
and finally to an absolutely necessary reformation of a theory of state.

First, it would mean the involvement of theoretical debate, and the
progression of research into the still confused field of *collective consumption*, i.e. socialised consumption processes which are largely determined by state activity. The fluid character of this concept, as well as the
poorly defined contours of the problematic, have at times been justly
criticised. This lack of precision is due to the absence of a sufficiently
elaborated theory for the understanding of a reality which is nevertheless highly differentiated at the level of social practice. It is widely
accepted that 'collective goods' are key factors in the economy and in
social organisation, without, however, this recognition being accompanied by a real analysis in terms of social relations. The point,
however, is not to entrench oneself into a purely formal conceptual
rigour which would paralyse this first stage of research. Bachelard has
reminded us of the experience of the epistemology of the sciences,
whereby the fecundity of a scientific concept is not so much related to
its identity principle as to its elasticity. This is the purpose of the current problematic on collective consumption. It is less important to

start from a complete theory than progressively to discover new concepts through the interrelation of three areas of analysis: the transformation of the capitalist mode of production, in particular relations between production and consumption; the historical development of needs; and the transformation of the economic role of the state and the internal differentiation of the public sector. This line of development must be the first theoretical challenge which new urban research must answer.

Second, the study of social movements must be envisaged as a collective endeavour able to produce change in social organisation on the basis of change in the relations of force between social classes (seen as historical agents).

What are the internal articulations of these movements? What are the conditions of their formation and development? How are they able to arrive at a political level? How are they interrelated, in accordance with the contradictions determining them and the processes which specify them? Here, only a dialectical theory of reciprocal action between different elements of reality which refuse the formal distinction between structure and practice can set us on the right path to answering this question. We have attempted to go beyond our initial theoretical formulation in this domain by presenting an analytical framework of urban social movements which can take into account, at one and the same time, the underlying stakes, the elements which make them up, and the effects they produce. But this contribution must be located within a *general theory of social movements* whose debate is still largely floundering between structuralism and subjectivism.

Third, priority must also be given to the *study of the state as the expression of social relations*. It is now clear that the 'urban' is largely defined in advanced capitalism in terms of its interaction with the state. But what is the state? It is certainly not the neutral institution of liberal imagery, nor the variable result of a strategic interplay of undifferentiated actors; but it is even less the passive and direct instrument of the dominant classes as it is painted by a certain Marxist tradition. The state is the expression of society, and thus both the crystallisation of the historical process and the expression of contradictory social relations which are at work in each period and in each social formation. But while such a formulation, which is mainly rooted in the Gramscian tradition, is the most fruitful and flexible, it is still too general. In order to specify it one must be much more precise about the relations between class struggles and the state, and one must also stress the internal differentiation within the state, recognising its contradictions as well as its homogeneity, its diversity as well as its unity. If the theory of the state is to be reconstructed, and go beyond either pluralist empiricism or mechanistic Leninism, perhaps the most fruitful path to take is to begin by a *history of capitalist states* – which could identify class–state relations from the historical diversity of their formation. This is contrary to a tradition which has tended rather to reduce these differences to an abstract model (itself a concrete historical expression) which has been considered immutable for ideological reasons. Rather than a theory of state, one should seek to develop in the first stage of research a *theorised history* of states which would closely relate the differential interventions of these states on the urban contradictions.

These needed theoretical perspectives must all refuse to consider what are seen as two major obstacles to the construction of a scientific theory of the city: on the one hand, the refusal to consider space as a given; and, on the other hand, the refusal of a purely economistic approach to social reality. Space in itself has no meaning because it is socially constructed – a similar spatial form may have very different social meanings. Urban social sciences must therefore move away from a spatial empiricism, precisely in order to carry out empirical research into the spatial expression of social relations. Furthermore; this analysis must take into account the whole social structure, and in particular the importance of class political relations, without, however, reducing the domination of capital to a purely economic process, to a moment in circulation, or to the unique expression of the profit search. This is because capitalist society is not constituted by capital itself but by a contradictory and complex social relation whereby capital structurally dominates only in the last instance, and only in an unstable manner. If the historical problematic is the way forward for the development of a new urban science, it can be done only through a kind of scientific research and analysis which would have to come to terms with these questions and solve considerable methodological problems.

These methodological problems are essential to research progress, but they cannot be posed abstractly in relation to a formal model of scientific rigour. They can only be understood in relation to general theoretical tasks which are themselves derived from questions which arise from practice. According to our experience, case studies have been very fruitful – as long as they are not monographs, but cases selected according to a sample of social situations defined in relation to principal hypotheses arising out of a general theory. This would entail a series of systematically programmed case studies, whose results could be articulated within a strategy of comparative research. In fact, within a theory which emphasises different historical processes, one must be able to relate social formations and historical periods according to relatively comparable issues. Thus the study of housing and planning policies, or of urban social movements within different political and historical contexts, would appear to be the principal avenues for a research which starts from the hypothesis of the growing role of urban contradictions in the process of social change.

Such a research perspective must make considerable progress in observational and analytical techniques, for more complex theories require more precision rather than more fantasy. But, at the same time, method must remain at the service of explanatory work rather than become a constraint forbidding further elaborations, or one aspect of the scientific approach is to accept the limits of each phase of research development, and to consider that we are now still in a phase which is largely intuitive and exploratory, rather than one of scientific discovery. At this point we can only talk of ideas and interpretations which are based on well-established empirical documentation which does not contradict interpretation. Instead of giving into methodological terrorism, we should accept the backward state of research into the fundamental questions of urban policy with `necessary modesty. This is not to be compliant to it, but one should advance slowly but surely through empirical observation and through the elaboration of a few hypotheses, which can be cumulative benchmarks towards a general theory of the city from the perspective of the process of social change.

This book sees itself as a limited and tentative example of such a project.

Notes and References

Chapter 1

1. We have given the reasons for such a theoretical and historical demarcation of the city elsewhere. We cannot summarise here the whole of our argument but its central thesis can be found in *The Urban Question* (London: Arnold, 1977). Let us simply say that we are not arguing that everything which takes place in cities centres around the means of consumption, but that the historical explanation of these urban problems and their specific definition originate in the qualitatively new role which these means of consumption play in advanced capitalism. See Chapter 2 of this text and the first part of our article 'Towards a Political Urban Sociology' in *Captive Cities*, ed. M. Harloe (London: Wiley, 1977).

2. For a more detailed discussion of this theme, see M. Castells, 'Theory and Ideology in Urban Sociology', in *Urban Sociology, Critical Essays*, ed. C. G. Pickvance (London: Methuen, 1975).

3. For our critique of pluralist theories applied to Urban research, see *The Urban Question*, part IV.

4. See the postscript to *The Urban Question*.

Chapter 2

1. For a theoretical and empirical argument along these lines, see *The Urban Question*, especially ch. III.

2. On the relation between urban organisation and life style, see M. Brooklin, *The Limits of the City* (New York: Harper & Row, 1973).

3. The analyses presented here will not be supported by statistical data but by reference to generally known social facts, but we accept from the start a certain *schematism* in this text; such is the price we must pay in sorting out the grand tendencies of social evolution to reach beyond the nuances connected with particular historical situations. We prefer to preserve in the proposed analysis its pre-emptory character, not trying to support and measure it by figures. Besides, the problems evoked here are too vast and too unknown for one to be, from a scientific point of view, as affirmative as we have been *for the sake of clarity* in our text. The attempt here is above all to present a certain number of *ideas* and *hypotheses* which can only be truly clarified by a series of concrete systematic analyses. It is hoped that these will have been made possible by the presentation of the general perspectives to which we address ourselves here.

4. For these analyses I refer to P. Boccara, *Etudes sur la capitalisme monopoliste d'Etat: sa crise et son issue* (Paris: Editions Sociales, 1973); Jean-Pierre Delilez, *Les monopoles* (Paris: Editions Sociales, 1972); P. Herzog, *Politique économique et planification en régime capitaliste* (Paris: Editions Sociales, 1972); P. A. Baran and P.M. Sweezy, *Monopoly Capital* (New York: Monthly Review Press, 1966).

5. For an analysis of this problem, see A. Granou, *Capitalisme et mode de vie* (Paris: Le Cerf, 1973), and for statistical sources which enable an appreciation of this transformation, the studies of CREDOC (Public Research Centre on Consumption Problems) on the consumption patterns of the French.

6. See J. Brière, 'La dialectique des besoins', *La Nouvelle Critique* (Apr 1974); and A. Heller, *La teoria dei bisogni in Marx* (Milan: Feltrinelli, 1974).

7. On the transformations of the utilisation of the work-force in relation to the new economic requirements, I refer to the general trends developed by M. Paci, applied by him in his study on Italy, *Mercato del lavoro e classi sociali in Italia* (Bologna: Il Mulino, 1973); see also F. Indovina (ed.), *Lo spreco celilizio* Padova: Marsilio, 1972).

8. See the problematic elaborated on this point by M. Freyssenet and F. Imbert, 'Mouvement du capital et processus de paupérisation', mimeo (Paris: Centre de Sociologic urbaine, 1973).

9. See J. P. Page, 'L'utilisation des prodiuts de la croissance' in Darras, *Le partage des bénéfices* (Paris: Miniut, 1966).

10. See the excellent work of J. O'Connor, *The Fiscal Crisis of the State* (New York: St Martin's Press, 1973), both for its analyses and the statistical and economic sources which are cited as a basis for his thesis.

11. See R. Stefanelli, 'L'intervento publico. Confronti internazionali', in *Le leve del sistema* (Bari: De Donato, 1971) pp. 263–84.

12. See the different sectors where public intervention become necessary in A. K. Campbell (ed.), *The States and the Urban Crisis* (New York: American Assembly, 1970).

13. We have allowed ourselves to use here, without repeating the basic concepts, works which have become classics in Marxist economic theory. For more information, we refer the reader to *Capital*, especially book III, section III, or, closer to us, the work of Bettelheim or the *Traite Marxiste d'économie politique* (Paris: Editions Sociales, 1971).

14. See N. Poulantzas, *Classes sociales et pouvoir politique de l'Etat Capitaliste* (Paris: Maspéro, 1968).

15. See M. Castells, *Luttes urbaines et pouvoir politique* (Paris: Maspéro, 1973).

16. See C. Palloix, *Les firmes multinationales et le procès d'internationalisation* (Paris: Maspéro, 1973).

17. We are familiar with the direct connection between the importance of multinational firms and the structural inflation of advanced capitalism; see C. Levinson, *Capital, Inflation and the Multinationals* (London: Allen & Unwin, 1971).

18. See J. L. Dallemagne, *L'inflation capitaliste* (Paris: Maspéro, 1972).

19. On the relationship of determination between classes and the state, I rely on the precise, subtle and new analyses contained in N. Poulantzas, *Les classes sociales dans le capitalisme aujourd'hui* (Paris: Seuil, 1974).

20. I refer for some basic facts to the following works: M. Young (ed.), *Poverty Report 1974* (London: Temple Smith, 1974) especially ch. 7, by Peter Willmott, for England; F. Ascher and D. Levy, 'Logement et construction', *Economie et politique* (May 1973), and to the 'Rapport de la C.N.L. sur la situation du logement on France', Colloque de Grenoble, *La nouvelle critique sur l'urbanisme* (1974) for France; the statistics and sources assembled by Francesco Indovina in *Lo Spreco Edilizio* (Padova: Marsilio, 1972) for Italy.

21. See for France the analysis of C. Topalov, 'Politique monopoliste et propriété du logement', *Economie et politique* (March 1974).

22. For the basic facts, see C.I.E.C., *Le financement du logement en France et à l'étranger* (Paris: P.U.F., 1966).

23. On this point see the extremely important book of D. Harvey, *Social Justice and the City* (1973) especially pp. 55–84; for empirical evidence on the Paris region, see M. Freyssenet, T. Regazzola and J. Reter, 'Ségrégation spatiale et déplacements sociaux', mimeo (Paris: Centre de Sociologie urbaine, 1973).

24. See D. Combes and E. Latapie, 'L'intervention des groupes financiers dans l'immobilier', mimeo (Paris: Centre de Sociologie urbaine, 1973).

25. This point is fundamental and perhaps already proven in the present state of research, at least *for France*. We refer for this to the basic texts that we cannot review here in detail: S. Magri, 'Politique du logement et besoins en main d'oeuvre: analyse de la politique de l'Etat en relation avec l'évolution du marché de l'emploi avant la deuxième guerre mondiale', mimeo (Paris: Centre de Sociologie urbaine, 1973). C. Pottier, *La logique du financement public de l'urbanisation* (Paris: Mouton, 1975); E. Préteceille, *La production des grands ensembles* (Paris: Mouton, 1973); C. Topalov, *Les promoteurs immobiliers* (Paris: Mouton, 1973); D. Cornuel, 'Politique de logement dans le C.I.L. de Roubaix-Tourcoing, mimeo (Paris: Ministry of Equipment, 1973).

26. See P. Hermand, *L'avenir de la securité sociale* (Paris: Seuil, 1967).

27. G. Pierre Calame, *Les travailleurs étrangers en France* (Paris: Editions Ouvrières, 1972).

28. See, in this sense, the very pertinent observations contained in the study of F. Ferrarotti on Rome: *Vite di baracatti* (Naples: Liguori Editore, 1974).

29. See F. Piven, *Regulating the Poor* (New York: Harper & Row, 1971), for France, see the report by Magri on 'Le logement des travailleurs' at the Colloque de CERM in 1973 in *Urbanisme monopoliste, urbanisme démocratique* (Paris: Cahiers du Centre d'Etudes et de Recherches Marxistes, 1974) pp. 143–91.

30. See C. Petonnet, *Ces gens-là* (Paris: Maspéro, (1970); G. Heliot, 'Le logement des travailleurs immigrés', *Espaces et sociétés*, no.2 (1971).)

31. See E. Préteceille, *La production des grands ensembles* (Paris: Mouton, 1973) for the *ensemble* of sources and references on this theme. Very significant in the social logic of housing in France, we refer to the commented bibliographic synthesis by B. Lamy, 'Les nouveaux ensembles d'habitation et leur environnement' mimeo (Paris: Centre de Sociologie urbaine, 1971).

32. I refer for an analysis of the social bases of the transformation of housing policy in France to a text which caught this transformation at its beginnings: J. Bobroff and F. Novatin, 'La politique Chalandon: nécessité tactique et stratégie de classe', *Espaces et sociétés*, no. 2 (1971).

33. See the classic work of R. M. Fisher, *Twenty Years of Public Housing* New

York: Harper, (1959), as well as the very interesting inquiry of L. Kriesberg, 'Neighborhood Setting and the Isolation of Public Housing Tenants', in *Urbanism, Urbanization and Change*, ed. P. Meadows and E. Mizruchi (Reading, Mass.: Addison-Wedey, 1969) pp. 276–91.

34. An extreme case is perhaps the construction of the large housing project of Grande-Borne in Grigny, near Paris, by the 'official' architect of the French government, Emile Aillaud. He was commissioned to construct there, in the name of decor, petrified forms of his personal fantasies. Under the pretext of artistic creation, he has imposed his personal psychic universe on the life of several thousands of families who violently object.

35. C. Bettelheim has made the greatest efforts in this direction, especially in his book *Calcul économique et formes de propriété* (Paris: Maspéro, 1969).

36. The best analysis we know of this sort of problem is that of I. Szelenyi and G. Konrad, 'The Social Conflicts of Underurbanization', Institute of Sociology, Budapest (unpublished) relative to Hungary; for China, we refer to the article of M. Luccioni, 'Processus révolutionnaire et organisation de l'espace en Chine', *Espaces et sociétés*, no. 5 (1971).

37. See in this regard the fairly new viewpoint of the development of the suburbs which appears in the collection of C. M. Haar (ed.) *The End of Innocence: A Suburban Reader* (New York: Scott, Foreman, 1972), taking up again in a forward-looking manner the themes that were introduced ten years before by R. Vernon in *The Myth and Reality of Our Urban Problems* (M.I.T. Press, 1962).

38. See F. Ferrarotti, *Roma, da capitale a periferia* (Bari: Laterza, 1971); J. Remy, 'Utilisation de l'espace – Innovation technologique et structure sociale', *Espaces et sociétés*, no. 4 (1971); D. Harvey, *Social Justice and the City* pp. 96–120.

39. See Jean-Noêl Chapouteau, Jean Frébault, Jacques Pellegrin, *Le marché des transports* (Paris: Seuil, 1970).

40. See for the basic statistics (American) the classic by J. R. Meyer, J. F. Kain and M. Wohl, *The Urban Transportation Problem* (Harvard University Press, 1965); and for a theoretical analysis of the question, N. Julien and Jean-Claude Veyssilier, 'Transports urbains et contradictions sociales', *Architecture d'auhourd'hui* (Paris) 1 (1974).

41. See the documents assembled on this problem by the Italian trade unions: *Una Nuova politica per: transporti. Atti della Conferenza nazionale* (Rome: Edizioni Sensi, 1972).

42. See the very concrete analysis concerning the social determination of the Parisian metro routes in A. Cottereau, 'Les origines de la planification urbaine dans la région parisienne', *Sociologie du travail*, no. 4 (1969).

43. See the detailed analysis of the logic employed at the R.E.R. in J. Lojkine, *La politique urbaine dans la région parisienne* (Paris: Mouton, 1973).

44. See a good summary of some important research in this field in J. F. Kain, 'Urban Travel Behavior', in *Social Science and the City*, ed. Leo F. Schnore, (New York: Praeger, 1968) pp. 162–96ff

45. See the statistics presented by R. Revelle, 'Pollution and Cities', in *The Metropolitan Enigma*, ed J. Q. Wilson (Harvard University Press, 1968) pp. 96–144.

46. See specific analyses and observations of this kind assembled by M. Bosquet in his *Critique du capitalisme quotidien* (Paris: Editions Galilee, 1973).

47. See M. Segré, 'Politique scolaire et aménagement du terriroire en France', *Espaces et sociétés*, no. 5 (1972) pp. 105–28.

48. See, for example, J. Ion, *Les équipements socio-culturels et la ville* (Paris: Ministry of Equipment, 1972).

49. See specific analyser and observations of this sort in *Urbanisme monopoliste, urbanisme démocratique*, cited above. This problem is approached from a different perspective by J. Rémy and L. Voyé in *La ville et l'urbanisation* (Brussels: Editions Duculot, 1974) especially in the first part.

50. For an analysis which is both concrete and theoretical of this type of history of urbanisation, we refer to *Monopolville*, to be published in translation by Macmillan.

51. See the analyses of social movements in *Espaces et sociétés*, nos 6, 7, 9 (1972 and 1973), as well as the following: C. Pickvance, 'On the Study of Urban Social Movements', in *Urban Sociology: critical essays*, ed. Pickvance (London: Methuen, 1975). E. Mingione *et al.*, *Citta e conflitto* (Milan: Feltrinelli, 1971); A. Daolia, 'Le lette per la casa', in *Lo sprees edilzio*, ed. F. Indovina; M. Marcelloni, 'Le lotte Sociale in Italia', unpublished (1973), G. delba Pergola, 'Le lotte urbane', *Archivio di stuch urbani et regionali*, vol. 3 (1973); M. Castells, E. Cherki and D. Mehl, *Sociologie des mourements sociaux urbains. Enquete sur la région parisienne*, 2 vols (Paris: Ecole des Hautes Etudes en Sciences Sociales: Centre d'Etude des Mouvements Sociaux, 1974). I. Borja, *Estructura urbana y movimientos urbanos* (University of Barcelona, 1974).

Chapter 3

1. See H. Lefebvre, *La révolution urbaine* (Paris: Gallimard, 1970).

2. See certain contributions in the Colloque du Centre d'Etudes et de Recherches Marxistes, *Urbanisme monopoliste, urbanisme démocratique* (Paris: Les Cahiers du CERM, 1974).

3. See M. Castells, *The Urban Question* (London: Arnold, 1977), *Luttes urbaines* (Paris: Maspéro, 1973) and Chapter 2 in this book.

4. See M. Dagnaud, *Le mythe de la qualité de la vie et politiques urbaines en France*, unpublished Ph.D. thesis, Paris, 1976.

5. See the extremely relevant analyses of S. de Brunhoff in *Etat et capital. Recherches sur la politique économique* (Grenoble: Maspéro, Presses Universitaires de Grenoble, 1976).

6. Compare in this respect with the analyses of C. Bettelheim in *Calcul économique et formes de propriété* (Paris: Maspéro, 1969).

7. We are in fact not entering here into the debate around the collective or individual *use* of the means of collective consumption. We are refering to their production and management.

8. See F. Godard, 'De la notion du besoin au concept de pratique de classe', *La Pensée*(Dec 1972).

9. See M. Castells, E. Cherki, F. Godard, D. Mehl, *Crise du logements et mouvements*

sociaux urbains (Paris: Mouton, 1978).

10. See the very useful collection of statistics compiled by M. Freyssenet, F. Imbert, M. Pinçon, *Les modalités de reproduction de la force de travail* (Paris: Centre de Sociologie urbaine, 1975).

11. See the key work by P. Grevet, *Besoins populaires et financement public* (Paris: Editions Sociales, 1976).

12. See E. Préteceille, *Equipements collectifs, structures urbaines et consommation sociale* (Paris: Centre de Sociologie urbaine, 1975).

13. Most of our analysis is based on the fundamental statistical study by C. André, R. Delorme, and A. Kouévi, *Etude analytique des tendances significatives et des facteurs explicatifs de l'évolution des dépenses et recettes publiques françaises au cours de la période 1870–1970*, mimeo (Paris: CEPREMAP, 1974) 2 vols.

14. See C. Pottier, *La logique de financement public de l'urbanisation* (Paris: Mouton, 1975).

15. See N. Poulantzas, *Pouvoir politique et classes sociales* (Paris: Maspéro, 1968).

16. There exists a fundamental study which was not available at the time of our writing of this article, but which we nevertheless encourage the reader to consult, as it is the first comprehensive reflection of the problematic outlined here. We are referring to the doctoral thesis by Jean Lojkine, *L'Etat et l'urbain*.

17. See our self-criticisms in the 'Postscript 1975' of the third edition of *La question urbaine* (Paris: Maspéro, 1975).

18. See the collection of essays in the 'Colloque de Dieppe', *Politiques urbaines et planification des villes* (Paris: Ministry of Equipment, 1974).

19. See INSEE, *Fresque historique du systeme productif français* (Collection de l'INSEE, 1974).

20. See our analyses in the introduction of our book, *American Dreams and Capitalist Nightmares* (Princeton University Press, 1978).

21. See C. Quin, *Classes sociales et union du peuple de France* (Paris: Editions Sociales, 1976).

22. See N. Poulantzas, *Classes in Contemporary Capitalism* (London: New Left Books, 1975).

23. On the concept of 'reigning petty bourgeoisie', which is very useful in concrete analysis, see Poulantzas, *Pouvoir politique et classes sociales*.

24. See J. Sallois (under the direction of), *L'Administration* (Paris: Hachette, 1973); G. Martinet, *Le système Pompidou* (Paris: Seuil, 1973); Michel Crozier *et al.*, *Où va l'administration française?* (Paris: Les Editions d'Organisation, 1974).

25. See J. O'Connor, *The Fiscal Crisis of the State* (New York: St Martin's Press, 1973).

26. See D. Mehl, 'Les luttes des résidents dans les grands ensembles', *Sociologie du Travail* (1975) 3.

27. See J. Lojkine, *La politique urbaine dans la région parisienne* (Paris: Mouton, 1973; *L politique urbaine dans la région lyonnaise* (Paris: Mouton, 1974).

28. See F. Godard *et al.*, *La rénovation urbaine à Paris* (Paris: Mouton, 1973).

29. C. Topalov, *La SCIC, Etude Monographique d'un groupe immobilier parapublic*, mimeo (Paris: Centre de Sociologie urbaine, 1969).

30. See E. Préteceille, *La production des grands ensembles* (Paris: Mouton, 1973).

31. C. Topalov, 'Politique monopoliste et propriété du logement', *Economie*

et Politique (March 1974).

32. J. Bobroff and F. Novatin, 'La politique Chalandon: nécéssité tactique et stratégie de classe', *Espaces et Societes* (1971) 2.

33. See the unpublished study by M. Morville, *L'Intervention de l'Etat dans les équipements touristiques: le Languedoc-Roussillon* (Paris: Ecole des Hautes Etudes en Sciences Sociales, 1976).

34. On the practice of administrative impairments in matters of urban policy, see C. Topalov, *Expropriation et préemption publique en France (1950–1973)* (Paris: Centre de Sociologie urbaine, 1974).

35. See M. Castells and F. Godard, *Monopolville: l'entreprise, l'Etat, l'urbain* (Paris: Mouton, 1974). To be published in translation by Macmillan.

36. See R. Hill, 'The Urban Fiscal Crisis and the State Policies in the US', *International Journal of Urban and Regional Research* (1977) 1.

37. N. Poulantzas, 'L'Etat, aujourd'hui', *Dialectiques* (1976) 13.

38. See A. Gramsci, *Passato e presente. Quaderni del carcere* (Rome: Edition Riuniti, 1971) especially pp. 84–100.

39. See Mao Tse-tung, 'On Practice', *Collected Works* (Peking: Foreign Language Press).

40. See Castells, Cherki, Godard, Mehl, *Sociologie des mouvements sociaux urbains*.

Chapter 4

1. M. Castells and F. Godard, *Monopolville: l'entreprise, l'Etat, l'urbain* (Paris: Mouton, 1974).

Chapter 5

1. For a *theoretical* analysis of these themes, see our communication to the seventh World Congress of Sociology, Varna, 1970: 'Propositions théoriques pour une étude expérimentale des mouvements sociaux urbains' (Theoretical propositions for an experimental study of urban social movements).

2. The renewal programme is accompanied by two other operations, conservation and rehabilitation, which play a privileged role in certain historic quarters, such as the Marais. Their dimensions are, however, fairly small. We have limited ourselves to studying the renewal process itself, namely the demolition and reconditioning of a certain area in order to put up new constructions. Finally, to the extent that our aim is to grasp the logic of urban planning, we have left limited renewal operations based on purely private initiative aside.

3. It would be relatively arbitrary to treat Parisian renewal *en bloc* without distinguishing different *periods*. By carrying out a general analysis, we have placed the emphasis on the period centering around the 'Reconquest of Paris' and which drowns, under its weight, the first, very limited, period of 'Slum Renovation'; furthermore, a study based on the institutional mechanisms of renewal ought to distinguish, at least, a third period characterised by

the importance of private enterprise and of 'concerted action'. This last phase of the renewal programme does not, however, differ very greatly, *in its social content*, from the objectives of the 'Urban Reconquest'.

On the other hand, the unit of analysis (Paris) is justified by its historical and ecological specificity and, above all, by the utterly exceptional conditions of its administrative status, which enables us to see, in this particular case, certain urbanistic orientations *directly expressed* by the highest authority in the political apparatus.

4. The inquiry into the urban renewal of Paris was carried out, under our direction, by a team consisting of C. Dessane, H. Delayre, F. Godard, C. O'Callaghan, G. Puig and C. Škoda. A preliminary, partial account was given in *Sociologie du travail*, 4 (1970). The report on the research is published as F. Godard, M. Castells, H. Delayre, C. Dessane and C. O'Callaghan, *La Rénovation urbaine à Paris: structure urbaine et logique de classe* (Paris: Mouton, 1973).

5. For details of this analysis, see Groupe de Sociologie Urbaine de Nanterre, 'Paris 1970: Reconquête urbaine et rénovation – déportation', *Sociologie du travail*, 12 (4) (1970) pp. 488–514.

6. Construction of variables: (1) the *arrondissements* of Paris are ranked according to the values of each variable studied (*e.g.* proportion of Algerian Muslims in the population residing in the *arrondissement*); (2) the cut-off points of the distribution are determined, and by classifying the *arrondissements* in three classes (high, low, medium), a scale is obtained for each variable; (3) finally, each renewal operation is attributed to a class according to its location.

7. The quantified causal influence of each of the variables on the volume of the renewal programme cannot be established by simple, or even partial correlations, to the extent that all the variables are heavily inter-correlated. Consequently, the establishment of a 'path-analysis' model, which would be an appropriate tool for this measurement, comes up against enormous technical problems (with regard to the multiplicity of connections between a large number of variables) which we did not resolve.

8. The *District de la Région Parisienne* is an administrative authority depending directly on the Prime Minister.

9. This hypothesis, written in 1971, has been verified in 1977. Paris, transformed into a conservative stronghold, has been given local autonomy. Jacques Chirac, extreme right Gaullist, is the Mayor.

10. The *procédures d'action concertées* have been introduced to establish a decision-making process with the participation of the government agencies, public and private builders and private owners of urban land and of present and future housing.

11. The data derive from an unpublished study carried out in 1970–2 in collaboration with F. Lentin, at the Centre d'Etude des Mouvements Sociaux (C.E.M.S.), École Pratique des Hautes Études. We would like to thank her for her permission to reproduce this partial communication of our work. Given the themes and circumstances of the survey, we have systematically omitted all concrete details liable to permit any identification of the places or persons in question.

Chapter 6

1. I am referring particularly to my research with F. Godard, *Monopolville: the Corporations, the State and the Urban Process* (London: Macmillan, forthcoming) and to our current study on 'Collective Consumption and Urban Contradictions' in the United States, France and Italy during the period 1974–7.

2. M. Castells, E. Cherki, F. Godard and D. Mehl, *Crise du logement et mouvements sociaux urbains* (Paris: Mouton, 1978).

3. The research on housing has been published as Castells *et al.*, *Crise du logements*. There is also a research report on transport demands: E. Cherki and D. Mehl, *Crises des transports, politiques d'Etat et revendications des usagers* (Paris: E.H.E.S.S.–C.E.M.S., 1977).

4. D. Mehl, 'Les mouvements des résidents dans les grands ensembles', *Sociologie du Travail*, 2, 1975; E. Cherki, 'Populisme urbain et idéologie révolutionnaire dans les squatters de la région parisienne', *Sociologie du Travail*, 3, 1975.

Chapter 7

1. Statement from President Nixon in 'The Environment', *Fortune* (New York: Harper & Row, 1969).

2. B. Commoner, *Background Paper for the 13th National Conference of the U.S. National Commission for UNESCO* (New York: UNESCO, 1969).

3. P. Ehrlich, *The Population Bomb* (New York: American Reprint Co., 1976).

4. R. Neuhaus gives an excellent, somewhat caustic, description of this day in the centre of New York in chapter 1 of his *In Defence of People* (New York: Macmillan, 1971).

5. 'To Escape Ecological Disaster: International Socialist Planning', *Militant* (April 1970).

6. See M. Gellen, 'The Making of a Pollution – Industrial Complex', *Ramparts* (May 1970).

7. See, on this subject, the excellent collection of texts and experiences of the American revolutionary movement, B. Franklin, *From the Movement Towards Revolution* (New York: Van Nostrand, 1971).

8. See D. Nelkin, *Nuclear Power and its Critics: the Cayuga Lake Controversy* (Cornell University Press, 1972).

9. See, on this point, the *Report of the National Advisory Commission on Civil Disorders* (March 1968).

10. See M. Castells, 'La rénovation urbain aux USA', *Espaces et sociétés*, vol. 1 (1970).

Chapter 8

1. This has been quite clearly revealed in the case of France due to the development of research on urban policy. For a synthesis of the results of these researches, see the collective volume of the Dieppe Colloquium, *Politiques*

urbaines et plonification des villes (Ministry of Equipment, 1974).

2. See M. Castells, 'La crise urbaine aux Etats-Unix', *Les temps modernes* (February 1976).

3. See P. Grevet, *Besoins populaires et financement public* (Paris: Editions Sociales, 1976).

4. See E. Préteceille, *Equipements collectifs, structures urbaines et consommation sociale* (Paris: Centre de Sociologie Urbaine, 1975); and C. Pottier, *La logique du financement public de l'urbanisation* (Paris: Mouton, 1975).

5. This analysis has been further developed in 'State Intervention, Collective Consumption and Urban Contradictions' in *La crise de l'Etat*, ed. N. Poulantzas (Paris: P.U.F., 1976).

6. C. André, R. Delorme and A. Kouévi, *Etude analytique et numérique des tendences significatives et des facteurs explicatifs de l'évolution des dépenses et recettes publiques françaises au cours de la période 1870–1970*, mimeo (Paris: CEPREMAP, 1974) 2 vols.

7. See M. Castells, *La question urbaine* (Paris: Maspéro, 1972).

8. See M. Castells, E. Cherki, F. Godard and D. Mehl, *Crise du logement et mouvements sociaux urbains* (Paris: Mouton, 1978).

9. In the sense defined by Nicos Poulantzas in *Social Classes in Contemporary Capitalism* (London: New Left Books, 1975).

10. We are beginning to possess an important body of work on the empirical foundations of the determination of urban policies in France by the interests of monopoly capital; see, for example, J. Lojkine, *La politique urbaine dans la région parisienne* (1973) and *La politique urbaine dans la région lyonnaise* (1974), both published in Paris by Mouton.

11. See M. Dagnaud, *Ideologie urbaine de la technocratie*, unpublished Ph.D. thesis, Ecole des Hautes Etudes, Paris, 1976.

Index